Jazz and the Blues

Jazz and the Blues: A Remarkable Partnership

ISBN: 9798737504786

Jazz and the Blues: A Remarkable Partnership

Daniel Hardie

ISBN: 9798737504786

Dedication

To My Family

Contents

Introduction

"There was an outbreak of blues in every musical quarter. The ragtime craze followed. But jazz was still unborn.

Earl Chapin May

While the history of jazz is well understood, and considerable attention has been directed to the story of blues and its evolution, the connection between the two needs to be better understood. During the initial years of the Jazz Age many writers saw them as the same phenomenon.

Is that so, or was it true at that time? If they are so connected why have historians tended to specialize on one or the other, treating them as having separate histories.

Jazz histories have by and large treated blues as a characteristic of some performances or a type of composition. How they came to be, and their individual historical evolutions have been subject to scrutiny and comment in popular journals and in serious historical narratives. Who researched them and published narratives and what did they have to say about them or neglect to study? What did journalists and critics have to say about them in press and popular journals?

Writing for the Journal Popular Mechanics 1926, Earl Chapin May wrote an article headed:

> "WHERE JAZZ COMES FROM. Distinctive American Form of Music, an Accidental Discovery by Four Boys, Now Being Adopted into Classical Forms."

After pointing out that Johan Sebastian Bach used syncopation in a number of compositions he wrote:

> "When our south imported slaves, it also imported syncopation from Africa. When the dives of the old Barbary Coast of San Francisco introduced us to the one-step and fox trot they adopted a syncopation, developed in Buenos Aires, Argentina, which came from the tribal dances of Brazil. But the effects by which modern jazz is identified originated in our own southland and its Negroes.
>
> We first came to recognize them in the

Negro blues. W. C. Handy, an Alabama Negro, put the blues on our musical map. Handy was proprietor and manager of a dance orchestra. One night, more than thirty years ago, he was filling an engagement at the little town of Cleveland, Miss. Three local Negroes applied for permission to interpolate a selection. This permission granted, the trio, equipped with mandolin, guitar and bass viol, played, over and over again, a mournful primitive strain of twelve instead of the orthodox sixteen measures.

There were just three changes of harmony in this unfinished symphony, but it made a hit, partly because the guitar and mandolin players slid their fingers along the frets and produced the effects we now hear in the Hawaiian steel-stringed guitar and ukulele and partly because the bass viol player "wolfed" his tones. White folks present showered money upon the local Negroes.

Handy sat up and took notice. He studied the new type of music, which had a melody something like the Negro spirituals, but encouraged encores because if left the impression that there was something more to come. One result of Handy's study was the composition which has won fame as "The Memphis Blues."

This commentary raises clues important to our understanding of blues and jazz and contemporary perceptions of their nature. It raises the issue of the ancestry of the blues and detects jazz as having been played on the West Coast before 1917.

It also suggests a South American origin for syncopation and locates elemental blues in the American South in early colonial times.

It identifies the soulful qualities of the blues, the instrumental devices used to create them, and links these effects to early jazz.

There is much more in the article including an acknowledgement of the role of W.C.Handy in defining the blues.

That, and similar contributions to journals, published papers, and books afford an insight into the development of public perceptions about the origins of jazz and blues, whether we agree with them or not.

The present work will proceed on the assumption that they should be included where relevant to the historical narrative. Wherever possible the actual words of the contributor will be used.

There are many good histories of the blues, and of jazz, but I do not intend to cover the histories of either in detail. This work is concerned primarily with the conjunction of the two and of their mutual development. It is an unusual narrative in that it has to jump back and forth among historical periods and significant contributions to the understanding of the histories of each, as well as the changing attitudes to their development. Treating them in this way has provoked new perceptions of their individual beginnings and their developing relationship.

In doing so I have had to cover again ground previously traversed in my earlier publications. However, it differs in that I attempt to survey, in a short work, the whole history of two major components of Jazz History examining their beginnings, conjunction and their separate lives from first reported sightings to what appears may be an end to Jazz History.

———————————

"The negro loves anything that is peculiar in music, and this 'jazzing' appeals to him strongly. It is achieved in several ways. With the brass instruments we put in mutes and make a whirling motion with the tongue, at the same time blowing full pressure. With wind instruments we pinch the mouthpiece and blow hard. This produces the peculiar sound which you all know. To us it is not discordant, as we play the music as it is written, only that we accent strongly in this manner the notes which originally would be without accent. It is natural for us to do this; it is, indeed, a racial musical characteristic. I have to call a daily rehearsal of my band to prevent the musicians from adding to their music more than I wish them to. "

James Reese Europe

Chapter 1

Blues is Blues

'Is what it is, is what it is, is what it is.

Old English Saying

"Just what are blues?" asked Judge Carpenter.

"Blues are blues, that's what blues are," replied the professor.

Above: Record cover on rear side of the first 'Jass' recording.

The answer was written into the records and will stand as the statement of an expert."[1]

In April 1917 the world of popular music experienced a revolution when the Victor Recording Company released the first jass recordings to the market. Popular sentiment was divided, but the new music was a hit.

The previously unknown Original Dixieland Jass Band (ODJB) performed two tunes: *The Original Dixie Jass Band One - Step* and *Livery Stable Blues* - performances that introduced jazz and the blues and dazzled the record buying public.

The company announced that these pieces were original compositions by the band. This was quickly challenged.

They had to admit that the first side included a tune from an earlier composition *That Teasin' Rag*, and the copyright for *Livery Stable Blues* had previously been claimed by Alcide Nunez, a former member of the band. His claim became the subject of the legal action presided over by Judge Carpenter. The proceedings were in part reported, as above, in Variety Magazine.

The judge was voicing a question that was to become subject of much discussion. But there was also the unasked question: What is jass?

Presumably the Livery Stable Blues was jass. After 1917 it became jazz, but it was also blues. If asked what was introduced to the public by the ODJB recordings most knowledgeable people would probably reply jazz. But it was also the introduction of the blues to the mass market for popular recordings.

The Blues in the Jazz Age - an appeal to the African American Market.

They were linked. So much so that when the court was asked to decide the ownership of the song the judge had to ask for a definition of the blues. Jazz, too, has always been hard to define, and its meaning has been in dispute throughout its hundred years of life.

This work is about the answers, and about the links between their folk-based beginnings and musical developments that began in the urban dance halls of New Orleans before 1907 and persist.

The Blues Was the Blues

Blues was, to begin with, a country boy and jazz very much a city slicker, but the blues was to become part of the musical inheritance of the Jazz Age.

In 1916 the Folksong collector Dorothy Scarborough[2] sought to make some sense out of the blues:

"There are fashions in music as in anything else, and folk-song presents no exception to the rule. For the last several years the most popular type of Negro song has been that peculiar, barbaric sort of melody called "blues," with its irregular rhythm, its lagging briskness, its mournful liveliness of tone. It has a jerky tempo, as of a cripple dancing because of some irresistible impulse. A "blues" (or does one say a "blue?"-What is the grammar of the thing?) likes to end its stanza abruptly, leaving the listener expectant for more, though, of course, there is no fixed law about it. One could scarcely imagine a convention of any kind in connection with the Negroid free music. It is partial to the three-line stanza instead of the customary one of four or more, and it ends with a high note that has the effect of incompleteness. The close of a stanza comes with a shock like the whip-crack surprise at the end of an O. Henry story, for instance - a cheap trick, but effective as a novelty. Blues sing of themes remote from those of the old spirituals, and their incompleteness of stanza makes the listener gasp, and perhaps fancy that the censor has deleted the other line.

The Blues, being widely published as sheet music in the North, as well as the South, and sung in vaudeville everywhere, would seem to have little relation to authentic folk-music of the Negroes. But in studying the question, I had a feeling that it was more or less connected with Negro folk song, and I tried to trace it back to its origin."

What about Jazz ?

The origins of jazz were, in 1917, also obscure. Writing in 1917, Walter Kingsley, claimed by the NY Sun to be the greatest expert on the subject, wrote under the heading:

"Whence Comes Jazz?

Variously spelled - Jns, Joss, Jaz, Jazz, Jasz and Jascz."

"The word is African in origin. It Is common on the Gold Coast of Africa and in the hinterland of Cape Coast Castle. In his studies of the Creole patois and idiom in New Orleans Lafcadio Hearn reported that the word

"Jiz.' meaning to speed things up, to make excitement, was common among the blacks of the South and had been adopted by the Creoles as a term to be applied to music of a rudimentary syncopated type. In the old plantation days when the slaves were having one of their nine holidays and the fun languished some West Coast African would cry out, "Jaz her up," and this would be the cue for fast and furious fun. No doubt the witch doctors and medicine men on the Congo used the same term at those Jungle "parties". The sturdy warriors gave their pep an added kick with rich brews of Yorimbin bark that precious product of the Cameroons. Curiously enough the phrase "Jaz her up" is a common one to-day in vaudeville and on the circus lot. When a vaudeville act needs ginger the cry from the advisers in the wings is "put in Jaz," meaning add low comedy, go to high speed. To-day the Jazz bands take popular tunes and rag them to death to make Jazz. Beats are added as often as the delicacy of the player's ear will permit and accelerate the comic part as "hokum," or low comedy verging on vulgarity.

Low comedy verging on vulgarity

"Jasbo" is a form of the word common in the varieties, meaning the same Jazz music is the delirium tremens of syncopation. It is strict rhythm without melody. In one two time a third beat is interpolated. There are many half notes or less and many long-drawn wavering tones. It is an attempt to reproduce the marvellous syncopation of the African Jungle...... For years Jazz has ruled in the underworld resorts of New Orleans. There In those wonderful refuges of basic folklore and primeval passion wild men and wild women have danced to Jazz for gladsome generations.

Ragtime and the new dances come from there and long after Jazz crept slowly up the Mississippi from resort to resort until It landed in South Chicago at Freiburg's, whence it had been preceded by the various stanzas of "Must I Hesitate," "The Blues," "Frankie and Johnny" and other classics of the levee underworld that stir the savage in us with a pleasant tickle. Freiburg's is an institution In Chicago. If you "go South" you must visit that resort. It is worth-while though learned dancers there were slow in getting the complicated beats of the Jazz, but when they did, they went mad over the eery syncopation. Chicago likes Its pleasures direct, frank and unashamed. It likes smoke, and fresh bullock's blood, and the smell of the stock yards and the grind of car wheels on the margin of Lake Michigan, and it liked Jazz because it lent itself to intimate slow dancing. Now let me tell you when Jazz music was first heard on the Great Wine Way. I forgot to tell you that It has flourished for hundreds of years In Cuba and Hayti, and, of course, New Orleans derived it from there.

Now when the Dollys[3] danced their way across Cuba some years ago they now and again struck a band which played a teasing, forte strain that that put little dancing devils in their legs and let their bodies swing

spurred their lithe young limbs into an ecstasy of motion and mimicked the paprika strain in their blood until they danced like maenads of the decadence. They returned to New York, and a long time later they were booked on the Amsterdam roof for the "Midnight Frolic." and Flo said: "Haven't you something new - My kingdom for a novelty". And Rosie and Jenny piped up and said that in Cuba there was a funny music that they weren't musicians enough to describe for orchestration, their lips to humming and their fingers to snapping. Composers were called in; not one knew what the girls wero talking about; some laughed at this "daffy dinge music." Flo Ziegfeld, being a man of resource and direct action, sent to Cuba, had one of the bands rounded up, got the Victor people to make, records for him, and the "Frolic" opened with the Dollys dancing to a phonograph record. Do you remember? Of course, you do. That was canned Jazz, but you didn't know it then."

Critics are divided about Kingsley's slick elaboration of the roots of jazz, but it contains elements later to be established by research. The idea of African roots was to become a feature of later works about the origins of jazz. From the earliest days it was thought that it was somehow related to indigenous New Orleans music, but though the notion that it had come from Cuba was, at the time a new one, historians were to identify common characteristics between Cuban Music and that of other Spanish Colonies. Kingsley also recognised a link between folk music and the blues that predated the arrival of the first white New Orleans syncopated music in Chicago in 1915 and the earliest blues recordings.

———————————

Chapter 2

Jass – That Daffy Dinge Music

"Jazz is a style that can be applied to any tune. I started using the word in 1902 to show people the difference between jazz and ragtime. Jazz music came from New Orleans…"

Jelly Roll Morton[4]

In Chicago in 1917 nobody was really clear where the new jass music came from. Some knew that there was a band of New Orleans white musicians who claimed to have invented it. And there was Californian – Bert Kelly, who also claimed the honour. But what was the real story?

Walter Kingsley hinted at a dark African past transmitted to New Orleans through Cuba long before the first jass appeared in Chicago. This theme was seized upon by jazz historians in the 1940's. However, they were not able to demonstrate specific sources, nor channels through which it had been diffused. As I suggested in a previous work:

"It is evident from what we have seen of the music of the late nineteenth century that the lineage of jazz has to be sought first in comparatively recent times rather than a dim African past."[5]

Fortunately, research since the 1970's has revealed its place in the development of popular music and specific information about its appearance and growth in New Orleans. Though there is evidence of the appearance of New Orleans style dance music in California around 1908 there is insufficient evidence to support the proposal that jazz first appeared there.

The Emergence of the New Orleans Style[6]

It is not only possible to depict the musical influences that moulded the early jazz style in New Orleans, but also to identify many of the musicians who participated in its emergence and development, and to define the style with some precision.

In 1917 Walter Kingsley defined jass as:

> " a teasing, provocative monosyllable; it gets folks dancing, shimmying, swaying, finger snapping. The word has a rasp for the nerves that react in steps synchronizing with super syncopation."[7]

Syncopation is the quality most often cited in early attempts to define jazz. And it is at the heart of the matter. Between 1890 and 1917 New Orleans musicians shaped a musical format that was identified by its use of continuous syncopation. In 1916 audio research psychologist Professor William Patterson described it this way:

> "With these elastic unitary pulses any haphazard series by means of syncopation can be readily, because instinctively, coordinated. The result is that a rhythmic tune compounded of time and stress and pitch relations is created, the chief characteristic of which is likely to be complicated syncopation. An arabesque of accentual differences, group forming in their nature, is superimposed upon the fundamental time divisions."[8]

In 1924 composer Virgil Thomson proposed a more hard-nosed definition linking it with popular dancing:

> "Jazz, in brief, is a compound of the fox-trot rhythm, a four-four measure (alla breve) with a double accent, and a syncopated melody over this rhythm. Neither alone will make jazz. The monotonous fox-trot rhythm, by itself, will either put you to sleep or drive you

mad..."[9]

But of course, neither tells the whole story. The history of the development of such music in New Orleans is clouded by the fact of racial discrimination. New Orleans developed two forms of syncopated dance music - Black and White. Though the differences are slight they are of importance. It seems obvious that they must have sprung from the same source. However, there is little evidence of connection. Not much can be firmly stated about White Jazz before 1900, while the development of the Afro American New Orleans Style can be traced with some certainty.

Syncopated performance was not a feature of popular music in New Orleans before the beginning of the 19th Century. As in most of the nation, popular music had developed from Anglo Scots and European sources and by the 1890's included influences from folk and religious sources including a growing Afro American component. Small conventional orchestras of string and wind instruments performed popular music for dancing and other entertainments. This was also the tradition in New Orleans, though music in the city was tinged with French influence.

The Syncopated Evolution

Syncopation began to become a feature in Afro American popular dance music in the city around 1895. Before that it had been a regular feature in vernacular street music and other informal performances by small groups of string players and by groups of singers singing songs derived from folk sources of the black community.

A number of musicians who were interviewed by researchers commented on the change including Manuel Perez leader of the Olympia Orchestra, who was interviewed by Robert Goffin, and who nominated an orchestra that participated in the change. Here's part of the interview as published by Lawrence Gushee:

> "... In any event Perez was born in 1881 on Urquhart Street in the Seventh Ward. Just as he was beginning to learn trumpet, at age twelve, there was: 'a syncopated evolution.' Vocal groups composed of young creoles, or even of whites, such as those of the spasm band, 'retained the rhythmic aspect of all the badly digested music'.
>
> . . . At this time, his teacher, a certain Constant ["Coustaut"] who lived on St.

Philip Street had nothing but contempt and mockery for the "fakers" who went around from street to street. Two musicians were popular among the creoles and had a great influence on the young generation: Lorenzo Tio and Charles Doublet. Perez remembers that after 1895, even though they usually played polkas and schottisches, they [i.e., Tio and Doublet] let themselves be tempted by the infatuation of the audiences and went along with the new music. They constituted the link . . . between popular music and ragtime"

There's a lot more in this interview, but I have singled out this passage because of Perez's emphatic focus on the brief period 1893-1895 and on two specific musicians of the older school, Lorenzo Tio and Charles Doublet."[10]

This interview not only nominates the popular Tio-Doublet Orchestra as instrumental to the introduction of syncopated music but also links it with faking as a characteristic of informal street bands - the so-called Spasm bands believed to have been influential in the beginnings of both black and white syncopated performance. More specific information has facilitated identification of the links between this early syncopated music and the development of Afro American jazz.

The Tio-Doublet and Coustaut-Desdunes Orchestras were long standing traditional orchestras that played a part in the evolution of the New Orleans dance orchestra.

Here's how I listed some early New Orleans street performers in a previous work:

> "Fortunately, some of the musicians who participated in this informal music are known.

New Orleans street band before 1900, mandolin, guitar and string bass. The bass violin player is Albert Glenny who later played with Galloway and Buddy Bolden.

> There was the legendary harmonica player Blind Freddie, and the best known

of the Spasm Band performers was Emile 'Stalebread' Lacoume who formed a band of newsboy players performing on home-made instruments in about 1896. This group of white boys was known as the Razzy Dazzy Spasm Band. (Despite his Creole sounding name Lacoume is believed to have been of Irish extraction.)

In his youth Jelly Roll Morton belonged to a quartet of boys who sang hymns and spirituals for sandwiches and liquor at funeral wakes. He mentioned *Nearer My God to Thee* and *Steal Away* as items in their repertoire."

The band leader Louis Ned is believed to have played street music as early as 1869 and guitarist. 'Sweet Lovin' Charlie Galloway' performed street duet music with fellow guitarist Jefferson 'Brock' Mumford in 1885. Galloway also played street music with bass violin player Bob Lyons who began playing in the streets around 1885. Tuba player Wallace Collins also played with street music bands. These were musicians on the fringes of legitimate music whose influence on regular dance music was to be felt by the end of the century." Charlie Galloway's band of 1889 appears in the literature as the first to apply the new syncopated style to dance music, but historians have been reluctant to call it the first jazz band. Other improvising dance bands were also beginning to appear, notably a group led by Henry Peyton that included the brothers, cornetist Punkie, and trombonist Boul Boul Valentin. George Filhé confirmed that the Cousto-Desdunes Orchestra reluctantly played syncopated music in the early 1890's. The orchestra most commonly accepted as the first Jazz Band was that of cornetist Charles (Buddy) Bolden born in 1878,

| Charles Bolden family portrait

Recent evidence suggests that Bolden had been trained by Professor Walter Nickerson at Southern University.[11] Bolden began learning cornet around 1894 and was soon playing with Galloway's Band. He took over the leadership of the band in the mid

1890's. Bolden's band has been described by many witnesses as the first band to play what was later called improvised jazz and he has been celebrated as the first jazz cornetist. Bolden's achievement was to mix syncopation, and extempore performance with elements of Afro American street music, including blues intonation, with conventional dance music.

Jack Laine, a white musician, who was performing with string groups in the late 1880's, formed brass bands and later, small dance bands he said were performing in a ragtime fashion. Apparently, the Razzy Dazzy Spasm Band of 'Stalebread' Lacoume began playing improvised street music before 1900 that Lacoume believed was the first jazz music.

 Unfortunately, detailed information on the early history of white bands before about 1908 has not been published, though some descriptions from that time suggest an earlier beginning.

It seems that early in the twentieth century two forms (black and white), of a performance style known locally as swing or syncopation, had been established. Unfortunately, it was also called ragtime music, though it had little in common with the polished piano rags that became popular at that time. Though ragtime went on to become the dominant form of popular music, that came to an abrupt end in

1917, with the entry of white jazz into the national popular recording market, with the first Original Dixieland Jass Band recordings.

They were wild, fast, frenzied and had elaborate breaks. *Livery Stable Blues* which had originally been entitled *Barnyard Blues* featured extravagant instrumental breaks that sounded like the cries of barnyard animals, rooster, horse, and bull imitated by the frontline performers.

The Original Dixieland Jazz Band*

* The Original Dixieland Jass (Jazz) Band used mutes to create animal noises and other effects. The mute on the clarinet would appear largely ineffective. This was a staged photograph, of the kind that was used to create a whacky image, that was soon imitated to advertise most of the early recording bands.

These were the characteristics that Chicago and New York first associated with jazz. Almost nothing was known of its New Orleans Heritage at that time. Though African American bands from New Orleans had been performing in Chicago from around the same time as those from the white community, Henry Osgood, the first writer to attempt to create a history of jazz, did not include them in his work, writing in 1926:

> "Nowhere have I gone into detail about negro jazz bands. There are so many good ones it would be hard to pick out a few for special mention. None of them, however, are as good as the best of the white bands . . .There are fewer trained musicians and consequently more of the improvisations and variations which characterized early jazz . . . Many prefer them for dancing to the best white bands."[12]

Jazz (Jz) and Vaudeville

Beginning in 1914 the Original Creole Orchestra became the first Afro American New Orleans band to tour on the vaudeville circuit outside the city. They took the early New Orleans syncopated style throughout the states and even to Canada.

Leader, violinist James Palao, claimed that the Original Creole Orchestra was playing 'jaz' and Joan Singleton[13] found evidence that he had been using the term, at least as early as 1908 when the members visited the West Coast.

She found that he said he began using the term in New Orleans in 1905 when he was leading, the then celebrated, Afro-American Imperial Band. As she wrote: "the zz was added later", and he was the first to use the word to describe the music that came from New Orleans. As the group visited both California and Chicago, she argues that this adds substance to claims that the word was used in California before 1915.

It has always seemed peculiar that it was suddenly used by the white New Orleans' Original Dixieland Jass Band to describe their music. If the word was commonly used in New Orleans as some witnesses have suggested, it is no longer surprising that it appeared with them in Chicago in 1915. Some claims that it had been used on the Barbary Coast in 1914 may also be corroborated.

Regretfully we have no recordings by the Original Creole Orchestra or by its leader though after its disbandment Palao performed with other Chicago orchestras.

The first recordings by such pioneers of jazz did not begin until 1921, but little interest was shown by the record buying public who were largely unaware of the New Orleans origins of the, by then fashionable, jazz music.

_____

Chapter 3

Blues is Handy

"That was an origin of the blues, and the blending of the blues and ragtime created the jazz now prevalent, although the authentic composition, springing from the deeps of negro woe in haunts of urban vice, is seldom found in music shops.[14]"

Frank and Burt Leighton

Researchers who set out to trace the origins of the blues face a daunting task. Here's how I explained the difficulty in *The Ancestry of Jazz:*

"Partly this is because the blues is usually considered to be of recent origin, and partly it is because most of the ethno-musicological studies of blues musicians were conducted in the 1930's and later in the Mississippi Delta countryside. Many of those interviewed knew little of the early origins of the music and this work led to an impression, since promulgated by later writers, that the blues was created in that region. As was usual in that era the subject was also politicised and romanticised.

A later writer properly pointed out that the blues performers of the 1930's had been exposed to the blues of W.C. Handy and other published blues since 1912 and to commercially recorded blues since at least 1920. There is however substantial evidence of the blues being known before 1900 and comparative musicological studies suggest even earlier blues like music. Like ragtime, the blues suddenly became a part of published popular music in one year (1912) and the name 'blues' does not appear in published accounts before then. Like ragtime, too, the name was applied from the beginning to compositions that differed to some extent, and later it was applied to tunes that had little relationship to any of the conventional definitions of the form. As is often the case, such latter-day definitions often limit the opportunities we have to understand the family roots that branched out into the popular music styles of the twentieth century."[15]

The *Livery Stable Blues* was the first blues recorded by a jass band, and its association with jass embedded it in the mind of the public of the jazz age as 'the blues'. However, the blues had come to public attention before that. The tunesmiths of tin pan alley had been writing blues tunes since 1913 with the publication of *Nigger Blues*, and before that, well-known folk songs had a bluesy flavour.

Nigger Blues Popular song written by minstrel performer Leroy "Lasses" White (1913).Perhaps the first song published in 12 bar blues format.

George O'Connor - *Nigger Blues* 1916

https://www.youtube.com/watch?v=bh0PawLc3H g

In 1916 Dorothy Scarborough who began a search for information about the derivation of the blues pointed out that blues compositions had been widely published before that. She went on:

> "Negroes and White people in the South referred me to W. C. Handy as the man who had put the bluing in the blues. But how to locate him was a problem. He

had started this indigo music in Memphis, it appeared, but was there no longer. I heard of him as having been in Chicago, and in Philadelphia, and at last as being in New York.

Inquiries from musicians brought out the fact that Handy is now manager of a music publishing company, of which he is part owner, Page and Handy, and so my collaborator, la Gulledge, and I went to see him at his place.

To my question, "Have blues any relation to Negro folk-song?" Handy replied instantly, "Yes, they are folk music."[16]

Father of the Blues

Early in the twentieth century William Charles Handy had begun to establish himself as 'Father of the Blues' and as the composer of famed blues compositions. He supposedly began his musical education as a student of the organ but became a cornetist, band leader and composer, song writer, author and publisher. He also led a band for a minstrel group. He wrote that in 1905 in Cleveland he heard local performers playing local folk derived music and was prompted to compose blues music.

Handy was fortunate to be able to benefit from the emerging market for recorded music between 1900 and 1914.

His first blues - *Memphis Blues*, originally written as a campaign song (*Mister Crump*) for a local political candidate was retitled and published as the *Memphis Blues*.

It was recorded in 1914 by the Victor Military Band:

Victor Military Band - *The Memphis Blues*

https://www.youtube.com/watch?v=K13C-1I-Myk

His *St. Louis Blues*, sung by Bessie Smith, topped the Billboard charts in 1925.

Bessie Smith – *St. Louis Blues*

https://www.youtube.com/watch?v=3rd9IaA_uJI

One of the earliest recordings of *St. Louis Blues* was made by the Original Dixieland Jazz Band in 1921.

Not surprisingly Handy became a household word for the blues.

With the coming first jazz recordings in 1917, he began recording in the early jazz style, with his own bands, Handy's Orchestra from Memphis, Handy's Blues Band from Memphis (1919) and in the 1920's and 1930's as Handy's Orchestra and W.C. Handy's Orchestra.

Abbie Niles on Handy and the Blues

Abbie Niles, one of the most informed commentators of the 1920's met Handy and became intrigued with the man and the music. In 1921, Niles, writing in the journal New Republic, under the title Blue Note, pointed out the new place of the blues in popular music and commented on Handy's role:

> "The blues are one of the most interesting and significant examples of Negro folksong, but they wouldn't stay put. They broke through into American popular music; became confused with almost every related type; their origin forgotten, they have generally been passed over by collectors and students.
>
> ... The trickle of the blues into the national consciousness was started by

W. C. Handy (an Alabama Negro then living in Memphis and now his own publisher), the first of his race not only familiar with these weirds, but able and willing (racial reticence is peculiarly involved here) to set them down and write more in the tradition. Although, the title "blues" being commercially valuable, even with him it is not always an index to what follows, he has preserved some of the original examples in a very pure form, while some entirely his own, such as Beale Street, Saint Louis, Aunt Hagar's Children, meet every test of the folk-product except anonymity of authorship.

In writing down this music, he chose to represent the primitive treatment of the tonic third, in some cases by the minor, simple, sometimes by introducing the minor third as a grace-note to the major, or vice versa. The grin of the singers had been sardonic; the songs were as melancholy as their name would imply, but sadness in negro music is no more dependent upon the minor than is the colour of the sea upon pigment, and the blue airs demanded the prevailing major.

Handy's minor third, therefore, appeared as signifying a temporary change of mode, and it caught attention as none of the structural features (more important because indispensable) did. It acquired a name of its own: "the blue note." The more blue notes, the "meaner" the blues. And its occasional use, especially when immediately preceding a cadence, furnishes most white writers with their only excuse (from the historical standpoint) for having ever used the title "the Blues." There are not enough pedants, however, to preserve the integrity of the word at this late date. To Handy is also to be credited the introduction, in the accompanying bass of some blues, of the habanera or tango rhythm (a dotted quarter, an eighth and two quarter-notes), with a success explainable on the well supported theory that this rhythm - the native word is tangana - is of African origin. He also wrote in strange figures for the long line-end holds (lineal descendants of the echoing wails in the originals), which soon came to emerge through the mouths of saxophones or the crowns of derby hats as the jazz we know."

There are some interesting things in this appreciation of Handy:

(a) Handy acknowledged the folk origins of the blues.

(b) Niles set out the characteristic scalar form of the blues with modifications of the regular classical scale - blue notes - and what he called grace notes on the third and seventh notes irrespective of the chosen the scale. (Mi and La, in Solfa notation).

(c) There is an acknowledgement of the possible African origins of these variants

(d) Handy recognised a Cuban influence that appears to have inflected early New Orleans jazz and the Tangana rhythm that other witnesses said Buddy Bolden introduced to the blues of his time. In 1917 Walter Kingsley, rightly or wrongly, proposed this rhythm came to New Orleans through the Cuban Danzon and Orquestra Typicas.

Almost single handed Handy promoted the blues establishing it in the public consciousness before the discovery of jazz.

———————————

Chapter 4

Buddy Bolden's Blues

"Here's was among the first blues that I've ever heard
. . . happened to be a woman, that lived next door to
my godmother's, in the Garden District. Her name
was Mamie Desdoume. On her right hand, she had
her two middle fingers between her forefingers cut off,
and she played with the three. So, she played a . . . a
blues like this. All day long when she first would get
up in the morning.

The first blues I no doubt heard in my life."

Jelly Roll Morton.

Witnesses who had lived through the early years of
the twentieth century commonly said that the blues
predated the beginnings of jazz. Jelly Roll Morton
said that the blues was played by piano professors in
the bawdy houses of New Orleans before 1900.

New Orleans clarinettist Louis Nelson De Lisle born
in 1880 went further telling Alan Lomax:

"The blues? Ain't no first blues. The
blues always been."[17]

Morton commented that:

"even the rag and bones men would

advertise their trade by playing the blues on the wooden mouthpieces of Christmas horns – yes sir, play more low down, dirty blues on those Kress horns than the rest of the country ever thought of."

But the appearance of the blues in jazz like music coincided with the birth of syncopated dance music in New Orleans.

Buddy Bolden

Witnesses said that Buddy Bolden was the first to play the blues for dancing.

In 1968 one of the earliest researchers, Samuel Charters, produced a biographical dictionary of early black New Orleans musicians.

Here's what he said about Buddy Bolden:

"BOLDEN, CHARLES "BUDDY "

...Cornet; b. 1868, on 1st Street; d. Nov. 4, 1931; Baptist Buddy Bolden was a colourful, flamboyant musician, locally famous for "inventing" the hot blues". He and a guitar player, who lived in the neighbourhood, Charlie Galloway, worked out a few of the popular street songs for a small instrumental group and played them with the dance orchestras they were leading. Bolden himself played with strong, fierce power, and when he stood up in Globe Hall in the summer of 1894 and played an improvised instrumental blues in public, he was a sensation."[18]

The most famous tune attributed to Bolden is politely known as *Buddy Bolden's Blues*. Jelly Roll Morton introduced it in his celebrated interview with Alan Lomax at the Library of Congress:

"This is about one of the earliest blues. This is no doubt one of the earliest blues that was the real thing. That is a variation from the real barrelhouse blues. The composer . . . was Buddy Bolden. The most powerful . . . trumpet player I've ever heard . . . or ever was known. The name of this . . . was named by some old honkytonk people. While he played this, they sang a little theme to it. He was a favourite in New Orleans at the time.

(Plays and sings) :

I thought I heard Buddy Bolden say,

Dirty nasty stinkin' butt, take it away,

Dirty nasty stinkin' butt, take it away,

Oh, Mister Bolden, play.

I thought I heard . . . Bolden say,

Dirty nasty stinkin' butt, take it away,

Funky butt, stinky butt, take it away,

And let Mister Bolden play.

Later on, this tune was . . . I guess I have to say, stolen . . . by some author I don't know anything about. I don't remember his name. And published under the title of *St. Louis Tickler*. But with all the proof in the world, this tune was wrote by Buddy Bolden Plenty musicians know it.".

Funky Butt

Funky Butt is the most famous tune played by Buddy Bolden. Jelly Roll Morton thought Buddy composed it but actually it is a very old folk song (at least as old as the 1860's). In Buddy's time it may have been called *'Doin' the Ping Pong'*.

Lead sheet of *Funky Butt* transcribed by Paul Furniss.

Kinney's Hall aka Funky Butt Hall

Several witnesses suggested that the *Funky Butt* name was acquired in Kinney's Hall, an old Church that had   been converted into a dance hall. It was a hot night, and the hall was poorly ventilated; the crowd was sweating, and the atmosphere became foul.

. Trombonist Will Cornish improvised and sang new words about the smell. The song became known ever after as *'Funky Butt'* and the hall the Funky Butt Hall.

Jelly Roll Morton made several recordings of the song under the title of *Buddy Bolden's Blues* but several authorities including Sydney Bechet expressed the opinion that the Morton ensemble version was too slow.

Jelly Roll Morton (Piano) - *Buddy Boldens Blues*

https://www.youtube.com/watch?v=qSFr1S0z6dA

It also appears too nostalgic. However, in view of evidence that Bolden's Band did not play very fast numbers a moderate blues tempo suitable for dancing appears appropriate. Possibly the band was playing for dancers doing the *Ping Pong*. Unfortunately, we do not know much about the dance.

Louis James' String Band made a recording under the title *King Bolden's Song* with the main theme containing fewer of the characteristics of Morton's personal style.

The Louis James' String Band - *King Bolden's Song*

https://www.youtube.com/watch?v=6rTuiWswSR
w

It seems clear that the band members sang the chorus, possibly together. A New Orleans journalist writing in the 1930's wrote that the real words were unprintable. Bearing in mind the meaning of the title, the following, compiled from various sources including Lorenzo Staultz (Bolden's second guitar player) would appear authentic:

> "I thought I heard Buddy Bolden say:
>
> Funky Butt, Funky Butt;
>
> Take it away!
>
> I thought I heard Buddy Bolden say:
>
> Nasty Butt, Stinkin' Gut;
>
> Take it away!
>
> And let Mr. Bolden play".

Alternatively, the third line could be varied to "Dirty nasty stinkin' butt take it away".

Origins of *Funky Butt*

As indicated above, Morton thought that the melody, an original Bolden composition, was later stolen by the authors of a rag called the *St. Louis Tickle* published in 1904. (The theme also appeared in ragtime composer Ben Harney's *Cakewalk in the Sky* published in 1899.) However, there are traces of it going back to the Civil War, probably having been carried to New Orleans by upriver boatmen:

> "I thought I heer'd Mr. Lincoln shout,
>
> Rebels close down them plantations
>
> and let all them niggers out.
>
> I'm positive I heer'd Mr. Lincoln shout,
>
> Rebels close them plantations
>
> and let all them niggers out,
>
> You gonna lose this war, git on your knees and pray,
>
> That's the words I heer'd Mr. Lincoln say."[19]

Here Bolden was "tapping into a developing blues tradition that was emerging from earlier vernacular shout-based practices."[20]

How it was Played

Contemporaries commented on Bolden's playing of the blues. Bill Matthews was particularly impressed by the correspondence between Bolden's playing and his religious background. He said that:

> "Buddy put things in the blues that created a spiritual feeling in the listener

just like in the sounds of the old Levee camps.

...he had a moan in his cornet that went right through you, just like you were in church or something...He was the sweetest trumpet player in the world...Louis Armstrong, King Oliver, none of them had a tone like Bolden." [21]

..."He found those things to put in a blues, like old levee camps and like that, makin' a spiritual feeling go through you. He had a cup, a specially made cup that made that cornet moan like a Baptist preacher" [22]..."...and on those old slow blues, that boy could make them women jump out of the window. On those old, slow, low down blues, he had a moan in his cornet that went right through you, just like you were in church or something...He was the sweetest trumpet player in the world....Louis Armstrong, King Oliver, none of them had a tone like Bolden." [23]

Bud Scott, too, thought that religion was a primary influence on Bolden's innovations:

"Each Sunday, Bolden went to church and that's where he got his idea of jazz music.

They would keep perfect rhythm there by clapping their hands...Bolden was still a great man for the blues-- no two questions about that...He was a great man for what we call "dirt music."

Notwithstanding the limitations of oral history there seems to be a general consensus that these reports accurately reflect Bolden's introduction of the blues into dance music. and the apparent link between his oeuvre and that of Baptist religious music in the South.[24]

The corollary is that, as his style of syncopated dance music had by 1910 developed into a form recognized as the source of the style renamed jazz in 1915, he was the first jazz musician. Accordingly, he was responsible for the first melding of jazz and blues. The blues may have been the older of the two, but since then they have been inextricable.

Authentic Performance of Funky Butt

In 2004 the present author embarked on a project to perform the music of the Bolden Era with authentic instrumentation and performance practice with the creation of the Buddy Bolden Revival Orchestra.[25] The Orchestra subsequently performed at jazz concerts and festivals and some recordings were made of concert performances. A selection of such items has been uploaded to a YouTube playlist entitled the Best of Bolden. You can hear such a performance of *Funky Butt* at the link below.

David Sager who has made a study of recordings of early jazz and their relationship with the music of the Bolden era suggested that listeners should prepare themselves for listening to early jazz recordings:

> "Here, I ask the reader to indulge me in a good-faith attempt to acquire a semblance of musical neutrality. Please consider these points
>
> > ▪ Suspend all notions about jazz – what it sounds like and who plays it – and begin to think. of jazz in terms of musical intent, rather than a style, or even a genre.
> > ▪ Turn attention to the fact that there was, back in the early 1900s, an unnamed type of dance music down in New Orleans that was born in the black neighbourhoods.
> > ▪ Note that musicians who played this sort of music called it ragtime, although it was not the formal piano ragtime of Scott Joplin.

Some said it sounded like "ragtime played by ear."

▪ The music – with a variety of names – was slowly unleashed to the country by both black, and white, bands performing in cabarets and on the vaudeville circuit."[26]

These suggestions appear to be relevant when listening to the Buddy Bolden Revival Orchestra playing *Funky Butt:*

Funky Butt - Buddy Bolden Revival Orchestra

https://www.youtube.com/watch?v=ZD96XRgNAc Q

Thus, the partnership between jazz and the blues began with the development of instrumental ragtime in the dance halls of New Orleans around 1900.

Chapter 5

Whence Came the Blues?

"More interesting humanly were the dirges and improvisations in rhythm more or less phrased sung to an intoning more or less approaching melody. These ditties and dirges were either of a general application referring to manners, customs, and events of Negro life or of special oppositeness improvised on the spur of the moment on a topic then interesting. Improvising sometimes occurred in the general class, but it was more likely to be merely a variation of some one sentiment".

Charles Peabody 1903

Around the end of the 19th Century, W. C. Handy and others recognised earlier folk blues as a source of inspiration. Musicologists and other researchers have identified blues like music in reports going back to the first days of slavery and in earlier folk music from English, Scotch and Irish traditional folk music. Historian Arnold Shaw gathered evidence from the careers of early blues singers and concluded that disruptive social and economic changes in the Reconstruction Era, after the Civil War (1868/77) led Afro Americans to look for a new form of expression. He believed that it had begun to formalise throughout the Southern states as Country or Folk Blues. He found evidence that the early blues was first heard between 1892 and 1903.[27]

Folk music researcher Alan Lomax attributed the emergence of black feeling and the blue notes to the painful experiences of the black community between 1870 and 1899.

That having been said, the concentration of researchers on the American and African roots of the blues has, to a sizeable extent, concealed other aspects of its genealogy, including clear connections with Anglo-Celtic traditions[28].

Musicologist Peter van der Merwe detected blues links with both British and African folk music and was able to establish that blues elements were already appearing in white American folk music in the 1890's at about the same time as the first black blues were emerging.[29] So, it appears the blues were the product of a folk tradition that had already absorbed African and Anglo-Celtic influences.

Folk Blues

Urban Street Band Musicians were not the only performers to develop the blues. Sad, lonely feelings, that were suffered in the countryside led to blues being performed by farm workers in the fields, labourers on the road, railway gangs and other workplaces.

The so-called Folk Blues has become widely known due to recordings by performers, black and white, from the Delta district of North Western Mississippi made since the 1920's.

Here's how the Delta influence is described on a website promoting the Delta region:

Blues in the Country

"For more than a century, the Mississippi Delta has been the emotional heart of it all. More famous blues musicians have come from this area than any other region (or state for that matter) combined. Today, you can still feel the authentic vibe of Mississippi Delta blues history."[30]

The Delta blues singers typically accompanied themselves with a guitar.

A great deal has been written about origins of the blues. The 1920's were to see a growing interest in the blues in the musical press. Historian Karl Koenig discovered an interesting piece from 1922:

> "Perhaps the most interesting article written in 1922 was the one in the Musical Courier of Nicholas Taylor of Sierra Leone entitled 'Jazz Music and Its Relation to African Music.' Taylor quotes the 'Negro Musician' of June 1921, of which he is in agreement. It is stated that ragtime has genuine art possibilities, and one should: "embrace, study, improve and utilize its value; teach its source, history and influence."
>
> Taylor also addresses the question of how far 'jazz' music is traceable to the influence of African music. He is very definite of opinion when he says that 'I shall leave out of consideration the question of idiom which at once decides that 'jazz' music is not African

music. The element of rhythm is more closely related to African music but there is much more syncopation found in American music than African music. Jazz is regular in its accents and the. rhythmical content of its bars; it is mostly 4 and 8 bar periods. All of these are foreign to the African and scarcely recognized. In African music the use of irregular rhythms (syncopation) is conceived differently and different in its use. His theory is that the rhythms and musical elements brought to America by the Africans went through a process of reduction. This was done to suit their new conditions, and, in the article, he goes through this process with several musical examples. Thus, he states that 'at the present time jazz has nothing more or less in common with African music.'"

Finally, the article on the origin of the blues brings to light the fact that the medium of vaudeville had a large part in bringing this new idiom of blues and jazz to the majority of the theatre going public (especially the white patrons).

The brothers, Frank and Burt Leightons, are said to have discovered the "Coon Song" (the first, Frankie & Johnny) and were the earliest singers of 'blues' known to vaudeville, working hard to get across the 'blue' their dependence on it almost as an act.

The Leighton Brothers

They have grown to be so strongly identified with "blues," it is expected of them, especially "Frankie and Johnnie," mentioned by them in the above article. But comparatively in recent vaudeville times the "blues" were a strange song style to an audience. A minute percentage of the audience knew what it was all about. The Leightons had to work harder in those days to get across the "blues" than now, when almost all popular song-singing turns, even to sister acts, are using one or more. The sister acts found the "blues" songs were easy to harmonize).

In summary, the year 1922 saw: the maturing of arranged jazz. The critics and music scholars were beginning to question the origins of jazz: where it began, why it didn't happen in Europe, the influences of this new type music, and the value of its content. 1922 was an important year in the history of jazz and seemed, by the tone of the articles appearing during the year, to be a pivotal year in its evolution."

This commentary raises a number of issues:

(a) The thesis that the blues and jazz had roots in African music is raised   and rejected. This idea, also mentioned earlier, by Walter Kingsley, permeated much of early jazz literature. Historian critic Sam Charters sought to verify the connection between African Griot music and the blues in a trip to West Africa in 1974. He found some similarity of expression - in particular what he called the texturing of the voice, but concluded that they were separate forms, each having been developed by exposure for a long period to a new culture.

(b) The role of black theatre in popularising the blues, largely ignored by critics, has recently been explored in some detail by researchers Lynn Abbot and Doug Seroff.[31] The Leighton Brothers had exposed this linkage in their description their experiences and introduced the coon 'song' as an artefact of the theatre in their article of 1922.

Bert Williams with his stage
partner George Walker

(One of the most successful vaudeville recording artists was Bert Williams who recorded *Unlucky Blues* 1920 in a style typical of the stage style of the time.)

Bert Williams – *Unlucky Blues*

https://www.youtube.com/watch?v=w xN9uLRPKCs

(c) It considers Jazz and Blues as an idiom. This is noticeable in a number of commentaries of the time. However, the roots of the blues and jazz have mainly been treated separately in historical narratives. It is apparent that the blues emerged as a product of various experiences during the period after the Civil War, so much so that, in a previous work, I proposed that:

> "... It is appropriate to speak of the ancestry of the blues family than the roots of the blues. Perhaps there is also something to the view that the blues not a specific form but a mode—a set of performance practice conventions that have since been incorporated in a range of popular musical forms from jazz to rock and roll."[32]

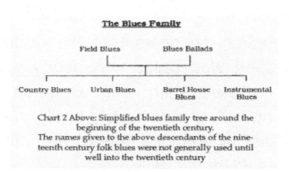

Chart 2 Above: Simplified blues family tree around the beginning of the twentieth century.
The names given to the above descendants of the nineteenth century folk blues were not generally used until well into the twentieth century

None of the above commentaries raised the issue of New Orleans jazz and its relationship with the blues

_____

Chapter 6

Recording the Blues

"Blues, being widely published as sheet music in the North as well as the South, and sung in vaudeville everywhere, would seem to have little relation to authentic folk-music of the Negroes." [33]

By 1917, when the first jass recordings were released, the blues had already received significant public attention. As previously indicated, black performers had been become more active in Vaudeville before the birth of jazz in New Orleans in the first years of the twentieth century. Blues soon began to be published by the tunesmiths of the time.

Recent research suggests that the earliest blues song published was called *I've Got De Blues* by vaudeville Artists Smith and Bowman in 1901. Another song with a suspiciously similar melody line was published by Anthony Maggio and published in 1908 entitled '*I Got the Blues*'.

Researcher Peter Muir considered that though the Maggio publication included a 12-bar blues sequence (which it featured in its first strain) it is

principally a ragtime composition in structure, and not a fully developed blues. He proposed that:

> *"The Blues"*, written by African American's Tim Brymn and Chris Smith, which was published as sheet music on 12 January 1912 was considered to be the first ever published fully formed blues and the one which initiated the popular blues music genre and the trickle of blues songs which soon became a veritable flood from 1916 onwards."

More traditional sources had indicated that the first blues published was the *"Dallas Blues"* written by Hart Wand and published in March 1912 then *"Baby Seals Blues"* by Baby F. Seals was published in

August 1912, and finally in September that year, W. C. Handy published *"Memphis Blues"*.

Early Recordings

Memphis Blues was recorded as early as 1914 by military style band – the Princes Orchestra:

https://www.youtube.com/watch?v=KnXpsC6YMS0

In 1916 a white minstrel performer George O'Connor recorded the first recorded vocal blues, the unfortunately named *"Nigger Blues"*. It was one of the first blues songs published. It was originally titled *"Negro Blues"*, but when published it in 1913, it was retitled .

George O'Connor – Nigger Blues

https://www.youtube.com/watch?v=bh0PawLc3H g

At around the same time, vaudeville singers began to record "blues" songs. Nora Bayes recorded *Homesickness Blues*, and Marion Harris recorded *Paradise Blues*, both in 1916.

Nora Bayes

At around the same time, vaudeville singers began to record "blues" songs. Nora Bayes recorded *Homesickness Blues*, and Marion Harris recorded *Paradise Blues*, both in 1916.

Nora Bayes-*Homesickness Blues*
https://www.youtube.com/watch?v=TEkoGPvWvhs

The First Instrumental Blues Recordings

The first jazz recording in 1917 encouraged a surge of copyist bands that recorded instrumental blues:

- W. C. Handy was quick off the mark, recording *Livery Stable Blues* in September 1917 as Handy's Orchestra from Memphis.
- The newly formed Frisco Jazz Band also recorded in 1917 with *Some Jazz Blues* as did Ford Dabney's Band, with *The Jazz – Lazy Blues*
- Wilbur Sweatman who claimed to be the inventor of jazz and blues recorded *Dallas Blues* with his Original Jazz Band in 1918.
- In 1919 a band of New Orleans White Musicians - The Louisiana 5 – recorded *Yelping Hound Blues*

Wilbur Sweatman's Original Jazz Band

Black New Orleans musicians did not enter this early recording spree. King Oliver's Creole Jazz Band remedied that with a number of blues records including *Riverside Blues* in 1923

King Oliver's Creole Jazz Band - *Riverside Blues*
https://www.youtube.com/watch?v=j_WbQYdQty 0

These early recordings were a whole new world, presenting a different face of the blues. Not the sad lonely musings of a depressed cornfield worker but a lyrical music tinged with blues intonation. The King Oliver recordings exposed for the first time the character of black New Orleans style jazz and its adaptation of the blues format to orchestral performance

Blind Lemon Jefferson

Country Blues

The early 1960's were to see the development of a growing interest in the Country blues among record collectors and critics, particularly in the delta blues recordings they, so avidly, collected.

Artists like Blind Lemon Jefferson became well-known and recordings by others like the fabled King Solomon Hill sought and treasured.

Many of those interviewed knew little of the early origins of the music and this led to an impression, since promulgated by later writers, that the blues was created in that region. A later writer properly pointed out that the blues performers of the 1930's had been exposed to the blues of W.C. Handy and other published blues since 1912 and to commercially recorded blues by artists like Bessie Smith since at least 1920. There is substantial evidence of the blues being known before 1900.

King Solomon Hill - *Tell me Baby*

https://www.youtube.com/watch?v=oo_M6gfDypk

We have heard that, at that time, artists like the Leighton Brothers:

> "conceived the idea of commercializing the pathetic lamentation of the unfortunates of the underworlds
>
> … that was an origin of the blues, and the blending of the blues and ragtime created the jazz now prevalent, although the

authentic composition, springing from the deeps of negro woe in haunts of urban vice, is seldom found in music shops."

… "Frank and Burt Leighton, now standard variety artists, belonged to a group of American minstrels, most of whom died young after going down into strange places to bring up the songs of negro outcasts, of cowboy, miner and gambler"

Black and White Blues

The Blues also became popular among white country recording artists early in the twentieth century, though recognisable differences in style between black and white performers can, by then, be noticed.

From a strictly chronological point of view the blues was first published by a white composer, and the first blues recordings were made by white performers. This accelerated after 1910 and, throughout most of the 20th century black and white performers of secular and sacred music shared a common tradition and repertoire. In the nineteen twenties white singers like Sam Mc Gee and bands like Bond's String Band were performing blues around the same time as the records of the black country blues singers were appearing. Jimmie Rodgers, known as The Singing Brakeman, included blues among his many

Jimmie Rodgers

Jimmie Rodgers - *Blue Yodel 1*

https://www.youtube.com/watch?v=h_JNVcTXnoI

recordings, entitled Blue Yodels. The white blues has since become a regular component of country music John Storm Roberts described the development of American music as a process of 'twin culture reinforcement' created when two cultures meet -the common cultural elements reinforcing one another so they continue to persist. Nowhere is this truer than in the birth of the blues

> "Though the influences on the blues are complex, the two major roots were the hollers of the field hands, freely structured and modal in character, and the ballads with their more disciplined eight and twelve-bar forms and conventional harmonic progression."[34]

Chapter 7

Blues Women

Stood on the corner with her feet all wet,
Begging each and every man she met:

Stood on the corner with her feet all wet,
Begging each and every man she met:

"If you can't give a dollar, give me a lousy dime,
I gotta feed that hungry man of mine."

"If you can't give a dollar, give me a lousy dime,
I gotta feed that hungry man of mine."

Mamie Desdoumes

1920 was to see the introduction of jazz-based vocal blues recordings to the growing jazz audiences and it was also to include, for the first time, Afro American performers. It started with a period of blues performance, dominated by women accompanied by Afro American jazz musicians, that stands out in the history of both the blues and jazz and began when Mamie Smith's *Crazy Blues* reached No.1 on the Billboard Charts in1920.

Mamie Smith and Her Jazz Hounds - *Crazy Blues*

https://www.youtube.com/watch?v=qaz4Ziw_CfQ

Mamie Smith and Her Jazz Hounds;
both Blues and Jazz.

Ma Rainey and other women blues singers also began to make recordings and in 1922 Bessie Smith's *Down Hearted Blues* reached No. 1 on the Downbeat Chart. Most of these performers were accompanied by jazz musicians and apparently New York experienced a shortage of accompanying jazzmen.

This was the beginning of a tradition of female blues performance that was to last through the Jazz Age and later days of jazz history, the era of Classic Women's Blues. As we have seen they were the first jazz/blues recordings beginning in 1920. Many of those recordings employed support from a jazz ensemble. Others performed with a pianist, unlike the guitar accompanied country Blues. Some writers consider it to be an amalgam of traditional folk blues and urban theatre music.

It seems appropriate that the beginning of recorded popular blues should almost exclusively feature a woman - the theme of many blues concerning her treatment by her man.

Ma Rainey

Ma Rainey

Stage and minstrel performer Ma Rainey, one of the earliest known blues singers, recalled that she heard the blues in a small Missouri town as early as 1902. She incorporated it in an act she devised with her husband Will Rainey, a song and dance performer. Their vaudeville show included both blues and popular songs toured the country, mainly in the South. They became popular in shows like Tolliver's Circus, The Musical Extravaganza and The Rabbit Foot Minstrels. She continued to tour into the recording era. In the 1920's she performed as a solo star on the T.O.B.A (Theatre Owner's Booking

Agency) vaudeville circuit for black artists. In 1923 she made her first recording for Paramount Records who billed her as Mother of the Blues.

Ma Rainey and her Georgia Jazz Band – *C. C. Rider*

https://www.youtube.com/watch?v=9duTAcatzlM

Mamie Smith

Mamie Smith

Mamie began working as a child performer with a white act, the Four Dancing Mitchells. As a teenager, she danced in the famed Smart Set show. In 1913, she left them and began working in clubs in **Harlem**. She made one of the first discs by a black artist when, on February 14, 1920, she recorded *"That Thing Called Love"* and *"You Can't Keep a Good Man Down"* for **Okeh Records**, in **New York City** with white accompanying artists. However, as we have seen above, she made jazz and blues history as the first **African-American** artist to make vocal blues recordings, performing with black jazz musicians, and becoming known as Queen of the Blues . She also performed on the new radio medium and in movies.

Bessie Smith More popular than other contemporaries, Bessie became widely renowned during the Jazz Age. She was the most popular female blues singer of the 1920s and 1930s and was a major influence on fellow blues singers, as well as jazz vocalists.[1] Her recording of *Downhearted Blues"* with piano accompaniment by **Clarence Williams** on February 16, 1923 made number 1 on the Downbeat Poll. It sold 780,000 copies in the first six months, and eventually 2 million copies were sold.

Dubbed Empress of the Blues, her name became forever associated with Handy's *St. Louis Blues* which she recorded in 1925 accompanied by Louis Armstrong on cornet and organist Fred Longshaw.

Bessie Smith

Handy was so impressed by her record of St. Louis Blues he encouraged her appearance in a movie of the same name in 1929. She sang the title song accompanied by a huge group of performers - members of **Fletcher Henderson**'s orchestra, the Hall Johnson Choir, the pianist **James P. Johnson** and a string section. Jazz Age audiences were to hear a bevy of other black women artists recording jazz/blues items.

Jazz Age Women of the Blues

Collectors treasured recordings by artists like Alberta Hunter some of whom had begun careers in the music halls and who had the good fortune to take advantage of the Race Record marketing schemes

80

aimed at tapping an African American black market.

This trend cemented the relationship between black blues and the black jazz of the time, with recordings aimed at an Afro American audience. These recordings were avidly collected by the growing number of white middle class collectors though black audiences were soon to move away from the style.

Marion Harris

There were few white women singers recording the blues in the jazz age. Established recording artist Marion Harris made what was probably earliest jass vocal - *"When I hear that Jazz Band Play"* issued as early as November 1916.Harris was probably the first woman to record a blues song with her *Paradise Blues* in 1916. She later left for New York arriving for a vaudeville stage show in early 1917. By then, the word jass had become accepted as the name of the new form of syncopated music. This link with the vaudeville stage may surprise some readers, but there were a number of New Orleans bands that undertook such tours.

W.C.Handy wrote:

> "she sang blues so well that people hearing her records sometimes thought that the singer was colored."[2]

Harris commented,

> "You usually do best what comes naturally, so I just naturally started singing Southern dialect songs and the modern blues songs."

Marion Harris - *Paradise Blues*

https://www.youtube.com/watch?v=PWwg3pk3_Y 0

Swinging the Blues

Throughout the 1920's recorded blues and jazz travelled comfortably together, despite the blues' dalliance in the Delta, but in the last years of the decade jazz began to move in a new direction of its own. The process began in around 1924 with the popularity of the softer jazz of the big bands led by

Paul Whiteman and others. Jazz began to diverge from its New Orleans roots. By 1929 women's jazz / blues singing also followed the trend away from hot jazz. Singers like Billie Holiday, Lena Horne, Memphis Minnie, Mildred Bailey each took popular song in new directions and its intimate partnership with jazz began to dissolve, though the blues itself, began to thrive in new forms.

Chapter 8

That Old Devil's Music

"The concept that a person may "sell his soul to the devil" is apparently rooted in both black and white American Folklore."

Gayle Dean Wardlaw

Though hymns, jubilees and shouts had religious intent, the delta blues were strictly secular. Some of the blue's performers went so far as to associate their craft with the devil. According to the myth Robert Johnson, one of the most celebrated singers, is reputed to have sold his soul to the devil 'at the crossroads', so he could play the blues.

The myth was furthered by recordings *'Hell Hound on My Tail"* and *"Me and The Devil Blues"*. All of this created the image of an earthy racy group of manly performers. The idea appears to have had its roots in a long-standing religious suspicion of the blues. This is how I commented on this in a previous work:

"Recent writers have pointed out that

blues songs, though popular among black audiences, were associated with the devil by the more religious members of their communities. Publicists used the idea of selling one's soul to the devil to promote the songs of early twentieth century blues singers like Charley Patton and Robert Johnson, neither of whom sadly appear to have reaped Faustian rewards from their bargain.[35]

Robert Johnson

However, this association appears to have had an earlier origin. The editors of Slave Songs of the United States recognised that their collection put together with the assistance of a

religious community in other parts of the South "fiddle songs," "devil songs," "corn songs," "jig tunes" and what not, are common; all the world knows the banjo and the "Jim Crow" songs of thirty years ago…. It is very likely that if we found it possible to get more of their secular music we should have come to another conclusion as to the proportion of the barbaric element"

There we have references to the ancestors of the corn-field hollers, ragtime and the blues all in one sentence. The Rev. Booker Miller told Gayle Wardlaw:

"Them old folks did believe the devil would get you for playin' the blues and livin' like that,"…

He confirmed that the idea of 'selling your soul to the devil' came from 'those old slavery times'. "The content of many blues songs certainly subscribe to the lifestyle envisaged by Miller's 'livin' like that'- fornication, brawling, gambling, lying and drinking, and even murder, feature prominently in twentieth century recorded performances.[36]"

While the women of the blues had experimented with the idea of jazz musicians, bands, soloists and pianists for accompaniment, their male counterparts invariably played their own on a guitar.

As the jazz age turned to Swing the women blues singers became part of the trend to big band formulae, singing in a smoother style, on commercially promoted recordings.

In the 1930's Artists like Lena Horn combined blues singing with a wider repertoire of popular songs.

Side by side with this trend, the commercial market

Mahalia Jackson

discovered gospel performers like Mahalia Jackson, and Sister Rosetta Tharpe, who accompanied herself on the guitar, dabbling with new models of guitar playing.

This was digging right back into a religious vocal tradition that opened up new avenues of style and content and Tharpe began to incorporate more secular aspects of love and sensuality into her recordings, an approach that was to become a feature of commercial recordings in the early 1940's.

In 1920 the African American audience for popular music was discovered by the big recording companies. Mamie Smith's Crazy blues was a hit. Believed to have sold a million copies it led to the marketing of Race Records aimed specifically at urban black audiences. At the same time that women's gospel was being transformed, male blues recordings were becoming more aggressive.

In 1933 the folk song researchers John and Alan Lomax discovered and recorded the guitarist, singer and gaol inmate Huddie Ledbetter later known to the public as Leadbelly.

Leadbelly.

He had an extensive repertoire of songs from the folk, popular and blues traditions and his own unusual style of performing on a twelve-string guitar. Over time he established for himself a place in the history of popular music as a harbinger of a more appealing and aggressive style of blues singing and guitar playing. Blues was becoming harder, more aggressive than ever. Leadbelly who styled himself King of the Blues wielded a large Stella twelve-string guitar, a veritable axe. He played with vigour and used a walking bass like the boogie woogie bass used by piano players of the time.

This approach to performance was to become a feature of male blues, with electrified instruments, that evolved into the Rhythm and Blues style as the decade moved on into the 1950's. By that time jazz was no longer at the center of popular music, being replaced by music that appealed more to a growing youth market.

Chapter 9

White and Indigo

"The blues are at their best as dance-music, but the orchestral treatment usually accorded them is a jazzing so continuous and indiscriminate that the melody is buried beneath the cowbells, rattlers and miscellaneous screeching machines. This is unfortunate because in many blues there is not only strangeness, but beauty, dependent only on a competent rendition. It may be a softly wistful beauty, or it may be the beauty of a savage and bitter power; this where it is jazzed, but properly, and without obliteration of its line.

Abbe Niles

Paul Whiteman has a unique position in jazz history. Not only was he an exceedingly popular star, having many hits at the top of the charts of the time, but his name has become synonymous with a larger orchestral format.

As a reviewer put it in 1924:

"When the five-piece jazz band was the "rage" it was always Whiteman's ambition to get away from the limitations which such combinations offered for turning out real music. He knew that it was impossible to create anything but jazzy ragtime effects with five men. And so, came into being the orchestras composed of ten or twelve men." [37]

Paul Whiteman and his Orchestra

In doing so he began to move the jazz of the 1920's away from its roots in New Orleans white jazz.

New York had never accepted New Orleans syncopated style dance music, having developed its own forms under the tutelage of Will Marion Smith and James Reese Europe. New York bands had never been limited to a prescribed   format.

James Reese Europe had an orchestra laden with six banjos, piano and one violin. Ford Dabney's Band had: Ford T. Dabney, piano; Allie Ross, violin: William Carroll, violin; William Parquette, mandolin; Charlie Wilson, cello; George Haywood, bass; F. Herrera, flute; Edward. Campbell, clarionet; Crickett Smith, trumpet; Fred Simpson, trombone, and Dennis Johnson drums.

By 1924 the public was ready for a revised format. In that year composer Virgil Thompson declared:

> "The instrumentation is not an essential element in jazz, as anyone knows who has heard a good performer play it on the piano.
>
> It is possible to employ practically any number or group of instruments, because, above the rhythmic accompaniment, which also sets the harmony, it is contrapuntal rather than homophonic and does not require balanced timbres. Certain instruments and effects. however, are characteristic, especially the use of the saxophone, which, in pairs or in quartets, makes a rich and penetrating diapason, and the monotonous banjo accompaniment,

giving out the ground rhythm - a rhythm so sonorous that it would be unendurable were not its hypnotic effect turned into motor stimuli by bizarre cross accents."

Whiteman, who was a well-trained orchestral musician had thought seriously about jazz and blues and their future. Here are some of the things he wrote about jazz and the blues:

> "Somebody, whose name has been lost to posterity unfortunately, declared illuminatingly that "Jazz is jazz and blues is blues."

> I feel a good deal the same way and so does anybody who knows jazz and blues. They explain themselves, but if you don't know them, words fail to clarify them. I have heard some folks refer to jazz as an "obnoxious disease," as a "musical profanity," "the true voice of the age" and the "only American art." You can readily see why I keep hedging. Who is going to find a definition to satisfy all these folks?"

He went on:

> ..."It is a relief to be able to prove at last that I did not invent jazz I took it where I

found it and I wish the preachers and club lady uplifters who put on sheets and pillowcases to go jazz-klanning wouldn't concentrate on me. I don't deserve it, really, nor the snorting editorials from Burma to Sydney, either."

..."All I did was to orchestrate jazz. If I had not done it, somebody else would have. The time was ripe for that. Conditions produce the men, not men the conditions. It merely happened that I was the fortunate person who combined the idea, the place and the time. At least, I think I was fortunate. Others are not so sanguine."

..."But to get down to business, jazz does seem to me to be, as nearly as I can express it, a musical treatment consisting largely in question and answer, sound and echo. It is what I call unacademic counterpoint. It includes rhythmic, harmonic and melodic invention."

..."To-day, however, jazz is a method of saying the old things with a twist, with a bang, with a rhythm that makes them seem new. Strictly speaking, it is instrumental effects. A large part of its technique consists of mutes being put in the brass. The first beat in any bar, which normally is accented, is passed over, and the second, third or even fourth beats are accented."

"...Jazz, which is ragtime and blues, combined with a certain orchestral polyphony which neither had, was still another way of letting off steam. At first, it was mainly rhythm running wild, tempos colliding with tempos. Yet syncopation and rhythm which were the distinguishing marks of the ragtime were not really new. And when you added counterpoint and harmony to the melody and rhythm of ragtime, you got blues, essentially a trick of harmony. But the blues were not new, either. Can anybody who has ever heard it forget the distant shore in the opening of "Tristan and Isolde" which shimmers in a blue haze that one can feel? "

The idea of orchestrating jazz and blues was not a new one. Whiteman pointed out that Handy had done so with blues compositions:

"...At first both ragtime and blues were a

sort of piano trick passed on from one performer to another. Up to the time that Handy organized an orchestra in Memphis, it is doubtful whether a single blue measure had ever been put on paper."

One of Whiteman's first experiences of jazz music left him excited but, by 1924, he felt the need for something more sedate.

His contemporary, the historian Henry Osgood wrote about the jazz he encountered "seven or eight years ago" - that is around 1919:

"The net result was, to sensitive ears the most nerve-harrowing, soul-wrenching noise ever produced in the name of music."

Though he did not pursue an interest at that time he changed his mind after hearing the modified form of arranged jazz in a hotel dining room; a performance of *Strolling Down the Lane* by Isham Jones:

"And there was no careless improvising in what the men played. Though most of them knew the music by heart, each one played a definite part that some clever musician had written for him in preparing the score."

Osgood was expressing a view growing among audiences - a reaction to what he called the 'gross extravagance' of some contemporary bands.

The time was right to tame the beast. Interestingly Osgood also linked the blues and jazz:

> "There is no necessity of connecting up the blues with the jazz, for they are jazz and nothing but – meatier, more primitive jazz than the rest of the product... Handy claims blues are the origin of all our modern jazz and considering their undoubted folk song origin, I wouldn't wonder if he weren't pretty nearly right".

Neither he, nor Whiteman, had apparently heard of Buddy Bolden, but Handy had already mastered the art of arranging the blues for his orchestra. xxx

The Triumph of Sweet Jazz

Whiteman forged ahead with the new style of arranged jazz developing the large orchestral format and proclaiming he wished to make jazz a new form of music comparable with more accepted classical styles. While he was not altogether successful in achieving that, he did cement its place as the most popular music of his time. Success led to acceptance that the large format he increasingly developed was jazz, though many still hankered after the five - piece white New Orleans Style, and a proportion of jazz enthusiast welcomed its transformation into the so-called Chicago style that has survived until today.

Whiteman did not make a feature of the blues, though most of his arrangements made use of the textural elements common to jazz and the blues and increased the use of blues resonances - sounds that had come north in the recordings of the ODJB.

Paul Whiteman's Orchestra – *St Louis Blues*
https://www.youtube.com/watch?v=_Afbr7tWCqs &list=LAK5uy_m4UT5lbFXk8QrllbGvhXHPFLS6K dvgxk

Whiteman was not alone. Many bands throughout the country quickly adopted the large-scale format and sought new formulae of expression some of which were borrowed from contemporary African American musicians.

In turn these bands began to adopt features of the big band style and developed still larger formats.

New York and the Big Bands

Commencing with its own established provincial syncopated styles, New York was also captivated, first by the big band music of Whiteman and his contemporaries, then by a New Orleans sound emanating from Chicago's black musical communities.

Many of the stars of early New Orleans black music first moved to Chicago, performing in resident orchestras, then moving to New York where their influence was felt by the local musical culture. In the process they found themselves adapting to the needs and traditions of those cities. Even Joe Oliver, traditional King of the New Orleans style felt the need to modify the composition of his band.

A disciplined team - Fletcher Henderson and his Orchestra

In the mid-twenties, New York began to develop its own style of Afro American dance music, using the saxophone choir as a major element of style. New Orleans stars were encouraged to perform as soloists, influencing the sounds of the ensemble. In particular their inherent use of blues intonation was borrowed and developed. Bands like Fletcher Henderson's utilized the big band format while adding their own musical inventions.

Fletcher Henderson's Orchestra - *Singin the Blues*

https://www youtube.com/watch?v=wZrry0o0Eik

By the middle of the decade a strong Afro American jazz idiom had evolved in the city employing orchestras somewhat smaller than those of Whiteman and his competitors. Henderson's performances combined disciplined arrangements and individual solo choruses taking advantage of blues intonation adapted to the characteristic sounds of each instrument. The saxophone choir featured, and emphasized glissandi derived from early jazz and blues. This created a swinging feeling that became known as Swing and marked a new era for Jazz and Blues.

White bands followed suit. Whiteman continued to be popular in the early thirties but, by1935, white big bands employing similar orchestral structure increasingly utilized big-name soloists in increasingly loud wild solos reminiscent, though somewhat more extravagant than, the showy techniques of the ODJB and its contemporaries.

Among them was Benny Goodmen virtuoso

clarinettist who developed the big band arranged jazz style throughout the decade stimulating increasingly larger and more spectacular imitators.

Benny Goodman and His Orchestra - *St Louis Blues*

https://www.youtube.com/watch?v=45Kx4KzfMn0

Though the blues remained part of the repertoire of the ever-growing expansive big band style it had become the junior partner though it was soon to demonstrate its power in the work of one of the survivors of the twenties.

In an Indigo Mood

The nightclubs of Harlem provided work for the new black bands of the twenties, none of them more than the black Cotton Club that catered for whites only.

In pursuit of talent the management offered a job to

Joe King Oliver fresh from Chicago. He refused and went elsewhere. This opened up an opportunity for a performer from outside the city. The Cotton Club traded on phantasy, an imagined atmosphere of the African heritage. Hence the name, but it was far from the cotton fields, with its 'sophisticated white clientele'. It was the ideal situation for Denver band leader Duke Ellington to let his imagination loose and he had a sophisticated musical imagination. The Ellington band could play in the popular style of the big bands, but he introduced a dose of the blues in a new form, utilizing the inherent characteristics of jazz instruments.

Duke Ellington and His Orchestra

Subtly, he took their hot tones and converted them to moody invocations of a black heritage. Smears and growls, long blue notes and other tones were used to color the melody red or blue or indigo. They were manipulated to produce sounds like a call in the night, or a lover's lament, images inherent in the Afro

American blues tradition. Mutes like the wawa mute were chosen and applied to amplify or mute the blue tones. In addition, carefully chosen tempos were introduced to create the required mood. At the same time Ellington kept up with the prevailing use of soloists performing complex patterns and demonstrating dazzling technique. The blues moved on to the centre of the stage in this arranged jazz formula. Ellington was not the King of Jazz, but he had rightly been installed as the Duke.

Duke Ellington and His Orchestra - *Creole Love Call*

**https://www.youtube.com/watch?v=o60EeEXbxH
s**

Duke Ellington and His Orchestra - *Mood Indigo*

**https://www.youtube.com/watch?v=GohBkHaHap
8**

Ellington maintained his style throughout the thirties and forties while keeping up with developments in both black and white big bands of the Swing Era. As time went-on he developed more sophisticated experimental compositions he considered outside the realm of jazz.

During that time other popular big bands dominated the charts featuring popular vocalists. They played continuously evolving riffs and complicated arrangements with virtuoso solo trumpet players playing ever increasingly complex higher and faster notes. The complex tonality of improvisations moved away from the standards of early jazz.

Brass choirs began to dominate recordings. Soloists began to introduce atonality to their performance. The music became more aggressive and over-confident with complex experimental combinations of instruments, and less emphasis on the sentimental melodic ingredients that led to the introduction of the big band in the 1920's.

No one expected jazz to cease to be the popular music of choice, nor that the blues might supplant it.

———————————

Chapter 10

The Latin Tinge

"They used a fiddle player to play the lead - a fiddle player could read - and that was to give them some protection... Buddy Bolden would say, 'Simmer down, let me hear the sound of them feet.' ... they'd shade the music...The rhythm then often would play that mixture of African and Spanish rhythm."

Danny Barker

In 1979 John Storm Roberts nominated Latin music as by far the greatest outside influence on the popular music styles of the United States. He proposed that in virtually all the major popular forms including jazz and rhythm and blues the major source of this influence was the music of former Spanish colonies like Cuba and Brazil.

Roberts identified the clave, the basic rhythm of the Habanera,[38] as the rhythmical foundation of post-colonial music in the Americas. In an interview for the Library of Congress Jelly Roll Morton verified the appearance of Spanish rhythms in the syncopated blues music of New Orleans commenting on his work New Orleans Blues:

> "That's the type of tune . . . was no doubt one of the earliest blues that was created as a composition . . . a playable composition . . . in the city of New Orleans. This tune . . . was wrote . . . about nineteen-two. All the black bands in the city of New Orleans played these tunes.
>
> . . . of course, you may notice the Spanish tinge in it. This has so much to do with the typical jazz idea. If one can't manage a way to put these tinges of Spanish in these tunes, they'll never be able to get the right season, I may call it, for jazz music. Of course, you got to have these little tinges of Spanish in it . . . in order to play real good jazz. Jazz has a foundation that must be very prominent, especially with the bass sections, in order to give a great background. Plus, what's called riffs today . . . which was known as figures. But figures has . . . hasn't always been in the dance bands.

I'll give you an idea what . . . this . . . the idea of Spanish there is in the blues."[39]

... But you must have a powerful background. For instance, those days they used *La Paloma* . . . was one of the great Spanish tunes.

Y'know, New Orleans was inhabited with maybe every race on the face of the globe. And of course, we had Spanish people, they had plenty of 'em. And plenty o' French   people.

Of course, I'll . . . I may demonstrate a little bit of *La Paloma* . . . to show you that the tinge is really in there.

Take it easy . . .

(Plays *La Paloma*)

That would be the common time, which it gives you the same thing in the . . .

I hope this is . . . quite clear to you, see. Only one is the blues but differentiating in these things. It comes from the right hand. You play the left hand just the same, but of course blues you . . . you . . . you get the syncopation in it. It gives . .

. an entirely different colour.

It really changes the colour from red to blue.

And maybe you can notice this powerful bass in the hand."

Roberts disagreed with Jelly Roll, arguing that the Spanish Tinge was, by no means absent from ragtime, pointing out that the exact structure of the rhythm varied from Spanish colony to colony.Numerous commentators have cited the influence of so-called Spanish Rhythms on early jazz. Commonly they refer to the syncopated tangana or habanera rhythm as an element of early jazz and blues.

The Clave in Recorded Jazz

Don Rouse explored such rhythmic influences in numerous New Orleans jazz recordings finding that both Caribbean music and New Orleans jazz contain what he called a 'multiple overlay of cross-rhythms' – rhythmic accents falling ahead or behind the regular meter.[40] He found that that guitarist Danny Barker said he learned this style of playing from Buddy Bolden's guitarist Lorenzo Staultz who also played in Frank Duson's Eagle Band. Barker wrote about Bolden in a number of publications and often stated that the Bolden band would play Spanish rhythms in soft passages when playing the blues.

Two Examples of the Clave

This was called Shading the Music. In later times it was called playing it tight. Danny Barker said Bolden told them to hush so he could hear the sound of the dancers' feet. As indicated above, Barker said that was when the rhythm section would play a mixture of African and Spanish syncopation. (A rhythm section riff perhaps).

John Storm Roberts noted that Barker's description:

> "...suggests the passages for percussion called rumbones that are still part of salsa today."[41]

On the other-hand, Baby Dodds said these Spanish Rhythms were not used by the Uptown bands when playing the blues but featured by Creole groups Downtown.

According to some witnesses sometimes after a number of these soft choruses they would "bust out loud" for the last chorus, and in some bands this last chorus was driven by the whole rhythm section playing all four beats of the bar giving the whole performance an extra lift. This is common practice today among traditional jazz groups all over the world.

In 1917, it will be recalled, Walter Kingsley wrote an account of the origins of Jazz in the NY Sun that located the origins of jazz in Cuba and Haiti and then associates its appearance in the   US with the commercial Vaudeville Theatre of the early 1900's, a proposal I suggested was   far from congruent with the received theory of origins derived from jazz histories written after 1930.

The Danzon and the Dolly Sisters

 As I suggested at that time, the then   popular, Orquestas Typicas, typically performed the Danzon, a descendant of the   Spanish Contradanza, was most likely the type of music the Dolly Sisters mentioned by Kingsley had heard in Cuba and it is known the Victor company made recordings there at that time.

Like the quadrilles performed in New Orleans around the end of the 19th century the Danzon included a number of dances.

The Dolly Sisters performed a highly successful dance act on the vaudeville stage, and they toured Cuba as early as 1906/1907, where they were very popular and became known as "Las Munecas Americanas" or "The Little American Dolls".

The Dolly Sisters early in their career (c.1910)

The Dolly Sisters performed in the Ziegfeld Follies of 1911 and 1912 and in the Ziegfeld, Midnight Frolics of 1916 and 1918.[42]

As indicated in an earlier chapter, in his first 1917 article, Kingsley described an incident that occurred while preparing for Florenz Ziegfeld's January 1916 Midnight Frolic at the New Amsterdam Theatre.

Ziegfeld asked performers to find a novelty to spice up the show. Kingsley wrote that the Dolly sisters suggested that they heard a "funny kind of music' in Cuba that made them dance frantically

Unable to find a local composer to write similar music for him Ziegfeld arranged for a Victor Co. recording unit to record a Cuban Orchestra in Havana and used the recording to open the Midnight Frolic, with the Dolly Sisters dancing to the recorded accompaniment. Kingsley averred it was 'canned jazz'.

Apparently encouraged by the result, Ziegfeld, for the first time, hired an orchestra of black musicians to support the entertainment in 1917 – Ford Dabney's Orchestra - an off-shoot of James Reese Europe's Society Orchestra.

Interestingly, from 1904 to 1907, Ford Dabney had been the official court musician to President Noro Alexis of Haiti 14, so he should have had some experience of Afro Cuban/Haitian Music.

Contacts between Cuba and New Orleans

It should be recalled that New Orleans was a Spanish colony throughout most of its early life. So, the existence of a Spanish component in the music of the city at the end of the nineteenth century is not surprising.

 The tormented colony of Cuba became a major channel for the spread of Spanish and African musical forms in the Americas. After extensive research into the role of Cuba as a hub for the dissemination of music between Africa Spain and the American colonies Neil Sublette made a persuasive case that there was considerable sharing of dance music in both directions between Cuba and New Orleans and the newly independent republic of Haiti.

Jack Stewart and others have also shown that there was continuous musical interchange between Cuba and New Orleans during the late 18th and 19th centuries. In fact, Cuba imported US performers from an early date.

In 1854 the New Orleans composer Louis Moreau Gottschalk performed on the island and he made numerous tours throughout the Caribbean and South America. He was deeply influenced by the music of Cuba and the Spanish colonies. Vaudeville too made its appearance in Havana. In 1903/4, for example, the Black Patti Troubadours led by the celebrated Concert star, soprano Sissieretta Joyner Jones, played in Havana, in the Caribbean and South America. Mme. Jones had been very successful on the concert stage and at some point, she became known as the 'Black Patti' – a soubriquet created by the press to suggest a voice comparable with that of the European Prima Donna Adelina Patti.

Sissieretta Joyner Jones
The Black Patti

Sissieretta Jones toured widely through the West Indies, South America, Europe and Britain.

In 1896 she formed her own Grand Concert Company that became known as 'The Black Patti Troubadours' and one of the most successful black road shows. The Troubadours travelled to Havana in 1904 and performed at the huge Grand Tacon Theatre on 19/21 March. It was reported that their receipts were greater than those of the Grand Italian Opera Company, Sarah Bernhardt and even Adelina Patti, who had earlier toured Cuba with Gottschalk.

There is no doubt that The Dolly Sisters performed in Cuba in 1906 nor that the Victor Company made recordings in Havana.

But what was it that was recorded there?

The Black Patti Troubadours

The Orquestas Tipicas

Popular dance music in Cuba between 1906 and 1915 was commonly performed by mixed instrument groups called Orquestas Tipicas that consisted of strings, brass and winds and usually tympani De Cuba (known as Timbales), commonly 2 Violins cornet, clarinet, flute, trombone, baritone horn, and 2 timbales. One of the best known of these groups was the Orquesta Flor de Cuba.

Trombonist Raimundo Valenzuela performed in the Orquesta Flor de Cuba. He took over the leadership and it became the Orquesta Raimundo Valenzuela.

After his death in 1905, its leadership was assumed by his cornetist brother Pablo and it became the

Above: Orquesta Flor de Cuba

Orquesta de Pablo Valenzuela that recorded for Edison, Columbia, and Victor.

Between 1906 and 1915 these Orquestas Tipicas performed the Danzon, a Cuban dance form that descended from the earlier Spanish Contradanza – a multi section dance format not unlike the Quadrilles common in turn of the century New Orleans. Apparently, they also performed some march-time numbers, and it was common to borrow sections from other compositions to fill out danzon performances:

> "Borrowing themes from pre-existing music and incorporating them into danzones became common practice beginning in the 1880s. Since the danzon achieved wide popularity among all sectors of society by the

Raimondo and PabloValenzuela

end of that decade, composers appropriated melodies from diverse sources including operas or symphonic music, traditional Afro-Cuban melodies (rumbas, carnival songs), guarachas and boleros, even foreign melodies from Spain, the United States, or elsewhere. The danzon's sectional form and use of contrasting multiple themes made this sort of appropriation easy. Raimundo Valenzuela (see Fig. 2.3) appears to have been the first arranger to adopt the technique, followed in short order by Enrique Pena, Felipe Valdés, Félix Cruz, 8 and others. Early examples of such melodic borrowing are found in two distinct Raimundo Valenzuela danzones, both entitled "El Negro

Bueno." 'The original song he took inspiration from, a guaracha by journalist and blackface stage actor Francisco "Pancho" Valdés."

Regrettably while there is an ample supply of recordings of contemporary Cuban ensembles no recordings of New Orleans orchestras have survived from the developmental period of Elemental Jazz between 1897 and 1917 despite the existence of recording facilities in the city. It appears that Buddy Bolden's Orchestra did make at least one cylinder recording but it has not survived.

How similar were the Cuban Danzon and the Elemental Jazz of the Bolden Era? Direct musical comparisons would appear difficult.

However, Historian Charles Suhor suggested the following criteria for identifying significant influence of Latin and other music on early jazz:

a. There must be a musicological likeness

b. There must at some time have been a close physical proximity of the musicians with early jazz players and/or their immediate ancestors

c. There should hopefully be some archived testimony from the early jazz players.

d. Anecdotal accounts can validly be part of c., but for credibility there should be some volume of quotes on a topic.

Musical Likeness

Here is how Madrid and Moore summarized the Orquesta Tipica:

> "'Cirilo Villaverde famously described popular dance venues of early nineteenth-century Cuba in his novel Cecilia Valdes, and orchestras consisting of violins, cellos, acoustic bass, and clarinet." But by the 1850s, following the invention of piston and rotary valves, cornets and low brass became a feature of such bands as well, and the ensemble later known as the orquesta tipica began to emerge. Various authors suggest that orquestas tipicas developed out of marching and military bands associated with the batallones de pardos y morenos (battalions of mulattos and blacks), segregated fighting units first established by Spanish colonial authorities in 1764. Carpentier describes one such band that included instruments now associated with the standard orquesta

tipica (such as the bassoon, clarinet, trombone, and bugle/cornet), as well as others (piccolos, French horns) that are not, at least in a consistent fashion." Similar ensembles of varied instrumentation are described as charangas in studies of Spanish military music.' Photographs show that the combination varied from group to group. A photograph of the Orquesta Henry Pena shows bass violin, two violins, flute, 2 clarinets, cornet, valve trombone, ophicleide, large and small timbales and guiro. 20. An earlier combination the Orquestra Failde contained: bass violin two

Above: Top left Guiro,
right Ophicleide –
Bottom left, Timbales

violins, cornet, two clarinets C and Bb, trombone, ophicleide and calabash like guiro. (No other percussion)."

This flexible combination of instruments is similar in many respects to those of New Orleans dance orchestras just before the Buddy Bolden Orchestra set the pattern for Elemental Jazz groups .

I have elsewhere commented on the similarity of the Orquesta Valenzuela's Danzon recordings made around 1906 and those of the King Oliver Band and other contemporary New Orleans Jazz Bands made after 1920. Valenzuela's recording of *La Patti Negra* (The Black Patti) a tribute to Sissieretta Jones[43] made in 1906 during Buddy Bolden's career is probably typical of what the Dolly Sisters heard. A tribute to the Black Patti, *La Patti Negra* has, in its second theme, an adaptation of the chorus of Cole and Johnston's *Under the Bamboo Tree*[44], a song that Sissieretta Jones performed during a tour of Cuba.

You can hear an excerpt from Valenzuela's version of *La Patti Negra at:*

https://folkways.si.edu/orquesta-pablo-valenzuela/la-patti-negra/world/music/track/smithsonian

At a conference for record specialists held in New Orleans Smithsonian researcher David Sager [45] commented on the similarity between the cornet style of cornetist Pablo Valenzuela and that of Fred Keppard:

> "It is generally agreed that Bolden's successor as the king of New Orleans hot cornetists, was Freddie Keppard. Keppard, whom we heard from earlier, played loudly, rhythmically, and with a rough edge.
>
> He also left behind enough phonograph recordings to give us an idea of his particular style. Amazingly Keppard's playing is foreshadowed in several dozen recordings made during the first decade and a half of the 20th century, by a cornetist not from New Orleans but in another port city located about 700 miles southeast.
>
> Pablo Valenzuela led his orquesta through the popular dances of the day, not quadrilles, but danzons, two-steps and waltzes:"

He went on to play examples for his audience that demonstrated the similarities. He chose the recording of *Here Comes the Hot Tamale* Man by Fred Keppard and his Jazz Cardinals - pressed in 1926 to demonstrate Keppard's performance style.

Fred Keppard and his Jazz Cardinals - *Here Comes the Hot Tamale Man*

https://www.youtube.com/watch?v=ZJDAWEqqb DE

Here, as a comparison; Yama Yama recorded by Orquesta Pablo Valenzuela in 1913 :

Orquesta Pablo Valenzuela – *Yama Yama*[46]

https://folkways.si.edu/orquesta-de-enrique-pena/yama-yama/world/music/track/smithsonian

What Sager did not say then was that witnesses considered Keppard to be the cornetist who most sounded like Buddy Bolden.

Apparently, there were a number of early New Orleans musicians who visited Cuba, including the members of the Onward Brass Band who joined the military, becoming members of a military band during the American invasion of Spanish colonial Cuba in 1896.

W.C.Handy who visited Cuba as early as 1900 wrote:

"The music of the island intrigued me. I never missed the concerts of the one-hundred-piece Havana Guards Band. More often I sought out the small, shy bands that played behind closed shutters on dark out of the way streets where the passionflower bloomed in the heart of the night. These fascinated me because they were playing a strange native air, new and interesting to me. More than thirty years later I heard that rhythm again. By then it had gained respectability in New York and had acquired a name-the Rumba."

He said, he introduced it into his own blues compositions - *St Louis Blues, Memphis Blues, Beale St Blues* and other works.

Early accounts of jazz history did not always neglect the effects of Latin styles on early jazz though there was some criticism that they largely framed the beginnings of jazz as a wholly North American phenomenon neglecting the French/Spanish Heritage of New Orleans. However, the Cubans were not the only Latin influence.

The Mexican Band Phenomenon

In 'The Ancestry of Jazz', I sketched influences from Mexico that may have affected New Orleans Music towards the end of the 19th century.

"The next major Latin influence to be felt in New Orleans appears to have come via Mexico. In fact, Mexican Music appears to have become something of a popular fad in the city. The culmination of a growing Mexican trend of the 1880's was the visit of the famous 'Mexican Band' that took the city by storm.

This was the visit of Payen's Eighth Cavalry Mexican Band to the World's Industrial and Cotton Centennial Exposition in 1884 where it performed to great acclaim. The band visited other US cities and returned to New Orleans in 1892 and again in 1898. Jack Stewart has pointed out that a number of other Mexican groups (Orquestas Tipicas) visited the city around the same time, in particular he mentioned a group led by Juventino Rosas. A number of Mexican musicians remained in the city as teachers and band leaders.

One of the effects of the visits of Payen's band was the publication in New Orleans of a stream of Mexican or pseudo-Mexican compositions, particularly those published by local publisher Junius Hart, and the Mexican Series of composer William T. Francis who had a close association with Payen's Mexican Band.

The best known of these publications was the Mexican waltz *Over the Waves (Sobre Las Olas)* written by Juventino Rosas and probably first performed at a Military Band concert at New Orleans' West End in 1890. The waltz was apparently a major feature of Mexican Music throughout the nineteenth century. Much of this so-called Mexican music was identified with Cuban rhythms, particularly the Habanera rhythm. This appears to have developed in Cuba from the French contredanse imported by refugees from a Haitian revolution in the early 1800's Roberts suggested that the blacks added a syncopation (or swing) to the rhythm of these Cuban contradanzas. He called it a lift. In this form it spread to Europe, Argentina and other Spanish colonies. He indicated that around the middle of the 19th century Mexican music became increasingly Cubanised and the Habanera form became widespread. The best-known example of the habanera is probably *La Paloma*, a tune that was very popular in Mexico"[47]

In this period a further influx of Spanish American musicians occurred. Mexican bands, Cuban or Spanish Orquestas Typicas and itinerant Spanish musicians appeared and there were a small number of musicians of Latin heritage. There was also a flourishing street music tradition.

The Spanish Tinge and Early Jazz

Spanish influences were still apparent in New Orleans around the time of the birth of jazz. Jazz musician Chink Martin recalled that:

> "Around 1895 he moved to Ursulines Street (the 600 block), across the street from what is now Brocato's Ice Cream Parlor. One of his fellow boarders was Francisco Quinones, who had come to the city as a baritone horn player with "The Queen's Own Band" from Spain.

The Spanish Fort Casino on Lake Ponchartrain where many early jazz musicians entertained the guests.

Quinones stayed on when the band left, and being an accomplished musician, began giving lessons to Chink. Chink remembers Quinones: "He was a heavy drinker, but that never affected his playing. He was a great guitar player and he played jazz."

Chink took guitar lessons from Quinones and learned to speak Spanish at the same time. At that time the area from Esplanade to Dumaine and from Royal to Decatur streets was populated mostly by Spanish and Mexican people....He experimented with mandolin, violin and banjo while with the Mexican band and remembers the music as being all "Spanish Style." They played for dances, but with a Spanish beat. The two-step was called "Pasa doble."In the early days of jazz there were a number of players with Mexican or other Spanish colonial ancestries and Mexican music also entered the US via California to make its presence felt in the later development of, so called, Cowboy music in the Twentieth Century.

Martin, who was taught guitar by a Spanish musician recalled participating in serenade performances before 1900:

> "He was playing guitar in 1898 for Spanish singers who would serenade their mothers or sweethearts late at night. Some of the songs were *La Paloma, La Calandrina* and a Puerto Rican song entitled *Cuba.* ...They serenaded people on the sidewalks and were often invited inside for food and drinks."

Beyond the Beginnings

The Latin influence did not die during the Jazz Age and continued to influence the development of new formats thereafter. By the 1940's South American melodies and dance rhythms had penetrated further northward into the United States The large bands of the swing era including the specialist Xavier Cugat began to feature repertory that included rumbas and congas, types of Afro-Cuban music Bandleader Stan Kenton, began combining the big band style and Afro-Cuban percussion with recordings of "The Peanut Vendor" and "Cuban Carnival" in 1947.

Xavier Cugat and his Orchestra

Ariba

However, jazz was changing too, and historian Marshal Stearns introduced the music of the Modern era with a nod to its Latin past:

"The sounds of bop were literally

unheard of and, accordingly, controversial. The very word seemed to give offense. At first, it was 'rebop', then 'bebop,' and finally 'bop.' Musicians said the word was an imitation of a typical sound in the new idiom. (The word occurs in the 1928 *'Four or Five Times'* by McKinney's Cotton Pickers, at the end of Chick Webb's 1939 recording of *'Tain't Whatcha Do,'* and in the title of Lionel Hampton's 1945 hit, *'Hey-Ba-Ba-Re-Bop';* but none of these recordings show any pronounced bop influence.) The likeliest source, suggested by Professor Maurice Crane, seems to be the Spanish expression 'Arriba!' or "Riba!' (literally: 'up'), which is the Afro-Cuban musician's equivalent for 'Go!' Such an origin would fit the known facts of the wide influence of 'Latin' music on jazz and its direct influence on bop."

Dizzy Gillespie, one of the leaders. of the bop revolution that combined Afro Cuban dance rhythms with bebop. Gillespie and Chano Pozo's musical synthesis became known as Afro-Cuban jazz or "Cubop." One of their collaborative efforts was the 1947 hit *"Manteca,"* which quickly became a standard   of the jazz repertoire.

Then this influence went on. As audiences evolved in the 1950s, big bands began to dissolve. What was called Afro-Cuban jazz and also   known as Latin Jazz began to be performed by smaller bands. Pianist George Shearing and   percussionist Cal Tjader were among the leaders of this trend in Latin Jazz on the U.S. West coast.

|Dizzy Gillespie

In the 1960's the importation of South American forms continued as the musical style featured by Brazilian Antonio Carlos Jobim — Bossa Nova arrived in the United States and was enthusiastically embraced.

These   and later Latin formats continued to be adapted and enhanced and Latin jazz continued its popularity and critical acclaim, and by the early 21st century it was still one of the most vigorous and components of jazz expression. Perhaps the influence of Cuban Music in continental America is best summed up by Ned Sublette[48]:

> "The history of Cuban music and its effect on American music has been largely unrecognized in the United States, perhaps for the simple reason that it was sung in Spanish. Cuban music was imported into the United States over and over again as a novelty, with campy costumes and horrendous stereotypes.

> Meanwhile, its profound impact on generation after generation of American musicians passed almost unnoticed. The problem was exacerbated after 1959, when Cuba became a sort of black hole in the minds of most Americans."

Influences from the music of early Spanish colonies added colour and rhythm to the music of Buddy Bolden and the blues of W.C.Handy and continue to do so.

Chapter 11

The Great Jazz Rift

"From the origins of jazz to bebop there is a straight line; but after bebop, the evolutionary lineage begins to dissolve into the inconclusive coexistence of many different, and in some cases mutually hostile, styles."

Scott DeVeaux

Quite suddenly around 1940 the word jazz changed its meaning. Two forces clashed – the continuing tradition of New Orleans Jazz and a new product known only by the title bebop. The latter was quickly redesignated Modern Jazz.

Historians have since tried to account for this sudden change. Two groups of enthusiasts emerged, those dedicated to the early tradition, and the boppers to whom the real jazz now replaced an earlier flawed and out of date jazz music. The jazz world was never the same again, and some jazz historians still find it difficult to bridge the gap. Is there a link that accounts for the appearance of bop or are the two forms so different they cannot be reconciled? Perhaps so, but which is the real jazz?

Barry Ulanov one of the prime promoters of modern jazz saw race as the link that joined the new tradition with original African roots proposing that slave dancing in New Orleans in the 18th Century, often linked with the development of early black jazz was the foundation of a joint tradition:

> "The effect of Congo Square was twice felt in jazz; once directly, as it filtered through the tonks and the barrelhouses, the Storyville parlors and ballrooms; again indirectly, when bebop musicians went to Cuba to reclaim their earlier heritage."

This romantic proposal suggests that the appropriation of the jazz tradition by whites in the Jazz Age needed to be reversed and that bebop was a reversion to the genuine African roots of the music.

Afro American musicians dominated the new music and brought it to fruition, but the extraordinary differences between the bebop of the 1940's and what we know about the syncopated music of the Bolden era, make the idea of a reversion to its genuine roots seem problematic.

Formerly celebrated musicians found bebop difficult to perform and were quickly considered out of date. There are comparisons with some of the extravagances of the late Swing period but the chromatic and technical differences between even Swing and bop are hard to explain, and historians have difficulty in accepting an evolutionary argument.

Charlie Parker

By the 1940's, differences between Swing and early New Orleans jazz were already so great that some enthusiasts were already rejecting Swing as real jazz.

Another interesting, and plausible, explanation of the birth of Modern Jazz is that this group of musicians was exposed to and influenced by modernist trends in classical music. They were well trained aggressively self-confident and belong to a group of assertive 'New Negroes' and music was dominated by these superbly proficient and imaginative Afro

American performers. Not attracted to earlier instrumental combinations they began with small groups led by the tenor saxophone accompanied by slap bass and drums, pianist and sometimes other wind players.

They composed new numbers often containing sly references to earlier jazz recordings.

Charlie Parker with Dizzy Gillespie - *A Night in Tunisia*

https://www.youtube.com/watch?v=gfLVVHxk4IM

Jazz had gone a long way since Buddy Bolden.

Notwithstanding reservations of lovers of more conventional jazz, bop was an immediate success and built an enthusiastic audience. Since 1940 its historical development has become generally seen by young musicians as the proper jazz, usurping other earlier forms.

In his study of the origins of bebop Scott DeVeaux identified possible roots within the late Swing Era but notwithstanding these links, he had difficulty accepting the idea that Bop was part of an evolutionary process.

However, he identified in the work of saxophonist Coleman Hawkins in the late Swing period, elements of formulae of jazz improvisation that came to fruition in the Bop movement.

The blue notes of early jazz became treasured sounds that bebop performers adapted to colour their performances, seeking new ways to utilise glissandi and sliding tones and mutes to tincture their individual expressiveness. The blues remained a component of the new jazz featuring in a movement to incorporate something of its atmosphere of sadness and deep feeling:

> "In the mid 1950s, the alto sax of Lou Donaldson was at the very centre of what was known as "soul jazz". The term was an attempt to acknowledge a particularly soulful and bluesy approach to the music - a groovin' feel which, to this day, makes Donaldson records quite essential for discerning club DJs. Tunes such as Blues Walk and Alligator Boogaloo, which rely so heavily on that swinging sax and organ combination have never ceased to be serious jukebox hits."[49]

DeVeaux proposed that Bop was a movement that changed jazz history and public perception of the music forever :

> "Bebop is a music that has been kept

alive by having been absorbed into the present; in a sense, it constitutes the present. It is part of the experience of all aspiring jazz musicians, each of whom learns bebop as the embodiment of the techniques, the aesthetic sensibilities, and ultimately the professional attitudes that define the discipline. A musical idiom now half a century old is bred in their bones."

He conceded that earlier favourites, like Duke Ellington and Louis Armstrong, enjoyed as much 'critical esteem' as the celebrated founders of bebop, and were better loved, and better known by the general public but:

"...bebop is the point at which we absorb the past at which our contemporary ideas of jazz come into focus. It is both the source of the present, 'that great revolution in jazz which made all the subsequent jazz modernisms possible' – and the prism through which we absorb the past. To understand jazz, one must understand bebop."

He is right, in that entrants to the profession are not generally aware of earlier jazz and its history, though they will certainly have heard of Louis Armstrong.

Names like Dizzy Gillespie and Charlie Parker have become enshrined in the pantheon of jazz greats and like earlier jazz Modern Jazz has evolved, each new development acquiring a following and a title - for example:

1940 Bebop

1950 Cool

1960 Hard bop

1965 Free Jazz

1975 Mainstream

1980 Neobop / New Swing

1990 Classicism

However, the appearance of bebop, and its acceptance by a professional cadre of informed expert performers, reinforced by the academicization of jazz education founded on a history of jazz beginning in the 1940's, was accompanied by the decline of public interest in jazz.

Recent commentators have begun to ask about what seems to be a difficult future for jazz. For example, one critic wrote:

"Perhaps one way to look at the form of jazz is that it has become almost a paradox - the whole point of jazz was to push boundaries of creativity and do what had not been done before. Yet how are jazz musicians supposed to create something entirely new if so much influence is on what has already been done? The "point" of jazz had, for a long time, seemed to be about pushing limits and playing with concepts of musicality. Today, jazz can seem mostly clichéd and concerned mainly with tradition and genres done before. Yet how are jazz musicians supposed to create something entirely new, if so much influence is on what has already been done? It is hard to look both forwards and backwards. Is it perhaps everything that could be done has already been done, and that there is no longer anything to create in an original manner?"[50]

During the later stages of the Swing Era popular music became dominated by popular songs played by lush large orchestras and, shortly after, new forms of vocal interpretation – a new style of popular folk singing - songs of protest.

Since then, there has been an overall decline in public interest in jazz music of all kinds, but the blues have marched on into a new and unexpected future. I have not gone into further detail here about the origins, history and future of bop. My objective was merely to set it in place in the history of jazz and blues.[51]

The word jazz had experienced yet another change of meaning and in a sense, this was the end of jazz as the dominant type of popular music.

Chapter 12

Guitar and a 'leccy Piano

"Music has a common characteristic that is unique to all cultures throughout the world. However, the music's form, or style, in every culture in history includes music as an important part of everyday life.'[52]

According to some jazz lovers jazz died during the 1940s, but then, the blues moved on to an independent life. In the early 1900's Buddy Bolden incorporated blues in the new syncopated instrumental music later called jazz, but the blues had a life of its own in New Orleans before that.

We have seen that W. C. Handy and Ma Rainey cited evidence of its prior existence elsewhere, including the townlands of the Mississippi Delta. While recorded jazz and blues was becoming popular in the 1920's, lone musicians in the South began making records with guitar accompaniment as described in an earlier chapter. The popular recorded jazz blues of the time was sung by Afro American women, but the Delta blues was an all-male affair. In parallel with the delta blues there was a strong gospel movement descended from the religious conversions of the Great Awakening crusades in the period 1790 to 1860, when slaves performed hymns and shouts in praise houses and outdoor assemblies.

Howlin Wolf

This vigorous approach to performance was to become a kind of male blues with electrified instruments that evolved into the Rhythm and Blues style as the decade moved on into the 1950's. By that time, jazz was no longer at the centre of popular music being replaced by music that appealed more to a growing youth market fed by highly produced performers like Chicago Blues player Howlin' Wolf who adapted R&B performance to suit the sensation hungry youth movement.

Richard Penniman, known as Little Richard, adapted elements of the shouts of the black churches to his rhythm and blues style. His adaptation of the blues made him a renowned pop singer. Later he was to return to religion becoming a traveling evangelist. Side by side with this development a stream of white blues performers began to dominate the popular white market. Elvis Presley emulated Leadbelly,

Little Richard

adopting much of his style and repertoire, and reached a vast popular following with huge record sales. The term Rhythm and Blues, apparently introduced by Billboard Magazine in 1947 to describe the early phase in the development of popular blues music was replaced by terms like R&B and Rock and Roll as the music evolved featuring a heavily amplified beat involving electrified guitars, now really known as axes, electrified pianos and other instrumentation.

Afro American artists, like B.B. King introduced a new vigorous loud style of solo electric guitar based on fluid string bending, vocal intonation and shimmering vibrato - wielding his instrument as another vocal

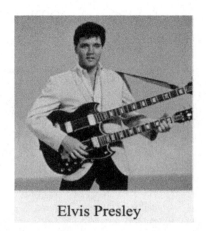

Elvis Presley

line, taking advantage of the ability of the instrument to produce glissandi and other elements of blue tone. Interestingly, King grew up with a holy roller church background. He sang in a gospel choir in a Baptist church and joined a Pentecostal church for its music, a fact rather reminiscent of evidence that: "Buddy Bolden put things in the blues that created a spiritual feeling in the listener just like in the sounds of the old Levee camps. ... he had a moan in his cornet that went right through you, just like you were in church or something"

It is not my intention to try to sort out this complex history as the words rhythm and blues have become an umbrella term for the form and its derivatives from 1940 to date; a transformation of what was folk derived blues into a vigorous kind of pop music that replaced jazz at the centre of a highly organised commercialised popular concert and recorded music industry - a form of popular music that spread to encompass international artists expressing youth's dissatisfactions and protests about life and oppression through the 1970's.

The Rolling Stones and Mick Jagger

International groups like the British Rolling Stones had great popular acclaim with a rather simplified musical format comprising electric guitar, bass guitar and drum kit. The emphasis was on the highly amplified vocal content rather than the similarly amplified accompaniment - a different kind of shout than its historical antecedents. The blues, like jazz, had changed though, becoming central to popular music at the time.

Chapter 13

Jazz is Blues, Blues is Jazz.

"There is no necessity of connecting up the blues with the jazz, for they are jazz and nothing but – meatier, more primitive jazz than the rest of the product."

It's hard to imagine a jazz performance that might not contain the characteristic sliding effect - gliding between the individual notes of the melody, that appeared in the earliest jazz recordings. However, the responses to the new music and the blues varied. The quotations in this chapter illustrate the varying perceptions of the time.

The first appearance of syncopated New Orleans music, soon labelled Jass in Chicago, also introduced a new form of orchestral blues to the local music scene. Here's how one journalist in Chicago described the appearance of Jazz music - labelled jass or jazz:

"In New Orleans the white people wanted

that certain rhythm to be played at their dances, and for a while they could not find enough coloured musicians to supply their demands. The white musicians at once started to try and play like the "Jigs," and finally there were many with a good ear and a fair understanding of music to not only equal but surpass the standard that was required to meet the demands of the dancing public. Still, they were known as dance orchestras. A would-be cafe proprietor, in order to outshine the lesser lights of the cabaret world, went to New Orleans and imported five white boys that were at that time engaged at the Pup Cafe. They set the town afire with noise and when the smoke cleared away it was found that they could not read but were a bunch of good fakirs. They were heralded as the "real Jazz band" playing "real southern Jazz." The "real southern Jazz" was nothing more nor less than a few of those darky melodies played as raggy as possible with each man slurring and making as many discords as they could while slipping and sliding to the melody of whatever they were trying to play.

The public went wild over them for a short while. It appeared strange that there were no musicians in Chicago that played the new kind of Jazz music. Someone asked for one of the latest popular melodies, and right there they died. The boys got together and started to playing all the "Blues" they could find and the result was that the public at once arrived at the conclusion that there were musicians right here that could play that wonderful Jazz music, hence the cabaret that has not a Jazz Band these days is not considered up-to-date, and the musicians that these Jazz bands are composed of are some of our best business musicians who are playing Jazz music and don't know it. The next Jazz Band you have the pleasure of hearing will convince you that my argument is plausible. They are like eggs. However, some good and some bad."[53]

The identification of the blues as jazz could not be clearer and - the writer proposed that discord was at the heart of both. The band to which he is certainly referring was that of Tom Brown - Tom Brown's

Band from Dixieland.

In 1915 it was this band, not the Original Dixieland Jazz Band, that brought the white New Orleans style

Tom Brown's Band from Dixieland dressed as The Five Rubes for a vaudeville show with dancer Joe Frisco

to Chicago. As is clear from the above comments, their performances caused quite a stir and their music was labelled Jass.

They later left for New York arriving for a vaudeville stage show in early 1917. By then, the word jass had become accepted name of the new form of syncopated music.

This link with the vaudeville stage may surprise some readers, but there were a number of New Orleans bands that took such tours.

Another element that produced discussion at the time was the emotional character of the blues. For example:

> "MISS GILDA GRAY'S "BLUES"
> AROUSE A DISCUSSION
> CONCERNING THEIR
> QUESTIONABLE ORIGIN.

> Listeners have sometimes thought that a blue must be founded on a negro spiritual. It has the musical character as well as the reflective nature of some of the negro hymns. Walter Kingsley says the missionaries did sing these hymns to the inhabitants of Beale and similar streets in the South in their efforts to change the ways of life that maintained there. Perhaps this was not accomplished so often as the good men and women hoped. But the hymn made its effect. It remained in the knowledge of the Negroes who had heard it shot at their ears in the attempt to make them better.

> "So, the 'blue' is the song of their aspirations and desires, good or evil,

and it assumes the form and sometimes the tune of the hymn, since that appears to Beale Street the only spiritual form of expression that ever came into its knowledge. The blue may be about an altogether unmentionable aspiration. It may on the other hand be expressive of a temporary piety. Sometimes the words of the missionaries and the desires of the singer become most incongruously blended, as in Miss Gray's song. As the 'blue,' which must inevitably be syncopated in tune and more or less affected by the rubato of jazz, comes to the public now, it mingles the voice of the dweller in the depths of Beale Street with the hoarse calls of the missionary to higher things."

Mr. Walter Kingsley, who has taken the time to investigate the origins of most of our distinctly popular American forms and methods in music, writes with some authority to the Sun on the origin of the songs of the underworld:

" 'Blues' are not for the expression of religious aspiration or the normalities of home and wife and mother. 'Blues' are not written to relieve the soul of church wardens, commuters, disciples of Dr. Crane[54], and the pure in heart of the theater. They are the little songs of the wayward, the impenitent sinners, of the men and women who have lost their way in the world. 'Blues' are for the outlaws of society; they are little plaintive or humorous stanzas of irregular rhythm set to music not of the conservatories. When one laments a season in prison one sings 'The Jail House Blues.'

For the girl whose 'sweetheart' of the dark alleys has gone elsewhere there are many blues, such as *'He Left Me Flat Blues,' 'Kidded Again Blues,'* and *'A Rat at Heart Blues.'* The forsaken male has his own repertoire, which includes *'Lying Skirt Blues,' 'She Done Him Dirt Blues,'* and *'He's Sore on the Dames Blues.'* The loser at craps, the luckless sport ruined by slow horses and fast women, the mourner for rum, the profiteer in things forbidden whom the law has evicted, the sick and lonely woman-all these have their appropriate blues. On the other side there are blues for luck at cards and women and horses, for big nights in the restricted districts, for pungent pleasures in the sectors of society that have no thought of the morrow; and again, there are blues with just a laugh for their object-low comedy fun in subterranean experiences. Just as Henley and Farmer's seven volumes of slang and naughty words covers the outlaw vocabulary of the English language, so do the blues embrace the outlaw emotions. They are right down on the ground in the matter of expression and packed with human nature and always interesting. As Wellington said, "There's no damned talk about merit' in them." They are gruff and sincere and as authentic as a ballad by Francois Villon." [55]

A Matter of Form

It's no secret that the blues is a composite of two musical elements. Most commonly it is composed of 12 bars (measures) of music, and it has its own scalar structure - at least that is an approximation of a correct definition.

The twelve-bar blues comprises three patterns of four bars and it is the blues form most well-known and widely performed. *The Livery Stable Blues* is a twelve-bar blues. So is *St. Louis Blues* though their emotional components are very different. To that extent *Livery Stable Blues* is unusual though not isolated. It is a fast instrumental blues without any deep emotional vocal component. Handy's *Memphis Blues* is another one though it originally had banal words that are long forgotten. *St. Louis Blues* is one of the slower more typical, blues of lament - with a woman complaining of her ill-treatment by her man who 'has a heart like a rock cast in the sea'.

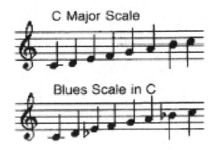

Example 1: The blues scale in C compared with the regular scale of C major

The Twelve-bar Blues has a long history and so does the so-called blues scale, referred to by early observers as discords. Technically, and approximately, the blues is played, whatever the key, with the third interval and the seventh of the scale interval lowered (diminished) by a half tone - the blue notes.

A Matter of Soul

I say approximately, because in practice, jazz musicians and blues singers do not hit the blue notes and sustain them exactly as written. Winthrop Sargeant, one of the first musicologists to attempt to analyse jazz performance found that blue notes were regularly incorporated in jazz performances. He described these notes as the variable third tones of each tetrachord in the octave:

> "Its' intonation is usually higher than that indicated by the flat before the note—i.e., somewhere between flat and natural—though the player often alters pitch during its passage, sliding up and down within the confines of this compass."[56]

He also quoted Abbe Niles who noted that Negro performers traditionally "worried these notes...slurring and wavering between flat and natural" [57]

This 'worried intonation' is an essential component of instrumental jazz. It cannot be articulated on the piano though some performers have been able to approximate it by lengthening or shortening the notes and expressive application of other pianistic effects.

Some early listeners grappled with the blues tones

as they began to become familiar to them as one of them described :

> "the few intermediate tones are quite as likely to be accidentals as to take other notes of the diatonic scale; indeed, the negro rarely sings the seventh note true, to a musical instrument, but generally flats it more or less as in the minor scales."[58]

Sorrow Songs

To begin with, white visitors to the South often commented on the sorrow in the songs of workers:

> "... there is no music among the South Carolina freedmen, except the simple airs which are sung by the boatmen, as they row on the rivers and creeks. A tinge of sadness pervades all their melodies, which bear as little resemblance to the popular Ethiopian melodies[59] of the day as twilight to noonday. The joyous, merry strains which have been associated in the minds of many with the Southern Negro, are never heard on the Sea Islands[60]. Indeed, by most of the Negroes, such songs as *'Uncle Ned'* and *'O Susanna'*

are considered as highly improper. In the schools, many of the best songs which are sung in our Sunday and public schools have been introduced and are opening new sources of pleasure to a race so musical by their very nature as are the Negroes of the South." - 1863

And again, more technically, in 1892:

"Genuine negro music is invariably in a peculiar minor, which differs from the civilized scale in two particulars; the sixth note of the gamut is omitted and the seventh is half a tone lower. Try over the specimen given above, making the F sharp, as it would be in modern music, and notice how completely the peculiar, plaintive charm vanishes. There are some other differences which cannot be represented in musical notation. For instance, the A in the fourth bar of the passage above in neither A nor yet A flat, but between the two. This scale is said to be that of primitive races-of the Esquimaux, the Egyptians, the South Sea islanders. Traces of it may be found in, Chopin and Grieg, composers who have made free use of volkslieder. I have no doubt that this music, like Voodooism, is a remnant of former idolatry. Doubtless many of these hymns have been sung for centuries before the shrines of fetishes in the dark jungles of Africa.

Some hearers began to collect and publish examples, like the song *"Keep Yo' House Clean"* shown   here, that clearly   conforms to the now classic 12 bar format and   with the traditional repetition of key   words in the vocal refrain. ".

Another example was quoted that emphasised the call and response pattern in the 12-bar structure and the emotional effect created:

"One very rare one, and one that I count among the best, is *"Cold Icy Hand*." The burden of the song is the response, "Death goner lay is cold icy hand on me." An indescribable effect is given to the "cold icy hand" by a syncopation. The word "cold" has the accent of the downward beat, and the first syllable of "icy" takes a half note in the middle of the measure. The surprise of the shock which this gives to the nerves, together with the weird tune which prepares one for any uncanny effect, is not unlike the touch of a cold hand. The effect is not less uncanny in the third line of the refrain, in an accidental flat or natural given to the word "cryin'." It is a wail like that of a lost soul."[61]

Hearing Jazz and the Blues

The analysis above introduces the issue that takes us to the very heart of the relationship between jazz and the blues, its evolution, and the public perceptions of audiences as they began to become familiar with the jazz of the 1920's:

> "The "blues" were a step in advance of "rag," declares Mr. Engel, for, whereas rag was mainly melody and rhythm, the blues were melody plus rhythm plus

harmony, but jazz has gone a step farther and to melody, rhythm and harmony, has added counterpoint."

Another writer went further into this historical development:

"Between the earlier 'rag' and the 'blues,' there was this distinction: the rag had been mainly a thing of rhythm, of syncopation: the blues were syncopation relished with spicier harmonics.

In addition to these two elements of music, rhythm and harmony, the people - who in the beginning had known but one thing: melody, fastened upon a primitive and weak harmonic structure of 'barbershop' chords – the people, I say, who had stepwise advanced from melody and rhythm to harmony, lastly discovered counterpoint. And the result of this last discovery is jazz. In other words, jazz is rag-time, plus 'Blues,' plus orchestral polyphony; it is the combination, in the popular music current, of melody, rhythm, harmony, and counterpoint."[62]

Not all music critics responded wholeheartedly to the combination, for example:

"The over-insistence of syncopation in both the primary as well as the secondary accents of a measure, the too tacit employment of transitional dominants and the frequent use of triple appoggiaturas in the bass before the principal accent of a measure (which, by the way, is more often than not given to the trombones in nearly all orchestral arrangements of "jazz" music by American Negro musicians, a serious abuse of that instrument), are the principal characteristics of a species of musical compositions which is called *Jazz Blues." "Mammy Blues," "Father Blues,"* and many other capricious names which the curious student fails to find in any musical encyclopaedic dictionary".[63]

Another educated commentator remarked on the improvised spontaneous inventions of the performers:

"These queer harmonies, mostly used in the "blues," are either invented by the composer or imitated from the accidental inventions of "ad lib," players of "jazz." They are often refined by the arrangers, but not entirely abandoned because of their characteristic nature. These "blues" came direct from the negro field hand, and were originally long-drawn wails, not, however, expressive of grief or discouragement, but, generally, of uplift and joy-often religious. But to the white borrowers of the idiom, they seemed blue, hence the name. Hence also, in imitation of the strange slurring and gliding of the negro singer at work (when he is unconscious of any listening ears), the so-called "blue note" in the arrangements (a diminished interval or minor note not belonging to the key) and the sliding harmonies with their frequent consecutive fifths, etc." [64]

And there you have it - blues is blues and jazz is syncopation and blues. A more 21st century commentary I found on the internet:

"An inside joke in the jazz & blues circles goes, "A blues guitarist plays 3 chords in front of thousands of people, and a jazz guitarist plays thousands of chords in front of 3 people." The main focus of jazz music is the dynamics and improvisations of an ensemble, while blues music is usually centered on a single guitar player/vocalist, and the personal lyrical content of the song. Most jazz tunes are purely instrumental, while a blues song always contains lyrics. Blues music was around before jazz and can be considered an element of jazz music. However, jazz would not be considered a part of blues music per se." [65]

It's from a long and comprehensive article, clearly a product of its time. I wonder if it's right?

———————————

Chapter 14

The Future and the Twins

"Blues is what cause the fellows to start jazzin."

Louis Big Eye Nelson

There is no doubt that the blues and jazz have always had an intimate connection. In an earlier work I proposed   that the blues had no name in the early 1890's:

> "the songs might then have been called ditties, but in the early twentieth century, under the influence of travelling black female singers and white publishers it became popularly known as the blues. Like ragtime it appeared around the turn of the century along with its new name and has dominated much of popular music ever since."

In Buddy Boldens' New Orleans, the new jazz music was seen as ragtime and because of its heightened syncopation musicians called it swing, a term that re-emerged during the 1930's as the big bands experimented with extensions of earlier patterns of syncopation and blues intonation.

The folk rags and ditties that were subsumed in the mainstream of the popular styles did not disappear. They continued to influence popular music throughout the twentieth century, a set of performance practice conventions incorporated in a range of popular musical forms from Jazz to Rock and Roll.

> "Ragtime represented the happy sibling in this folk family, but it had always had a sadder and deeper brother. " [66]

Jazz survives in the form of bebop and its derivatives.
In their publication Jazz, academic Scott De Veaux and journalist Larry Giddens described its situation:

> "- Jazz has now moved so far from centre stage that its survival is partly dependent on an infrastructure of academic study and institutional supports…

> - Jazz, and its musicians, are weighed down by the accomplishments of the past. Virtually every young jazz artist who

comes along is defined to some degree by the presumed influences of his or her predecessors..."

They suggest that in the period 1950-1970 jazz moved from its dominant position in the popular market by developing extremely modernistic styles that alienated the general public. As they put it:

> "Jazz became more of a listener's than a dancing music."

This form of jazz was adopted by academic institutions that began teaching curricula based on the bebop of Charlie Parker along with its developments since 1940.

In *Jazz Historiography* I commented on the difficulties expressed by later historians:

> "The arrival of Modern Jazz presents a new range of problems for our putative general history of jazz. There appears to be no shortage of information. The modern era has lasted over 70 years – apparently much longer than its predecessor but it still resembles its beginnings. If Marc Sabatella is correct the grammar of bebop has lasted despite various attempts at progress. As he put it:

"The styles of jazz discussed ...have become the common practice of jazz. They have been around for forty to fifty years or more, and they still form the basis for much of the jazz performed today. Most of the conventions of jazz music theory as discussed in this program were established by musicians playing in these styles."

DeVeaux also commented on the lack of consensus about the terminology used to describe later forms of modern jazz expression. Some of these included:

1940 Bebop

1950 Cool

1960 Hard bop

1965 Free

1975 Mainstream

1980 Neo bop / New Swing

1990 Classicism

Returning to the Past

Recorded jazz was always a listener's music that appealed to enthusiasts and collectors, some of whom became dissatisfied with the modern trend, anchoring their tastes in revivals of the past.

There were those that sought to return to the Jazz Age, emulating the white jazz of the Chicago or Black New Orleans performers of the 1920's, forming seven-piece bands to cater for the interests of an audience that revelled in recordings of the past.

Another trend fostered by journalists and history writers in the 1940s was stimulated by the evidence of some older New Orleans players, who had actually experienced or played early New Orleans' Elemental Jazz. They created revivalist bands and recorded interpretations of the original sounds of that era. This appealed to a world-wide audience and led to the formation of revivalist bands, as far from the source as Australia and Sweden, that are performing today and making recordings of traditionalist jazz.

There are also a widely diverse number of revivalist bands catering for a largely middle-class white audience. Afro Americans have shown little interest in revivalism except in New Orleans.
These revivalist performers black and white continue to cater for audiences and record sales believed to be declining as do those of bebop despite its academic supports.

Are We Seeing the End of Jazz?

There has always been a concern among its adherents that jazz might not survive, and in 1987, they prevailed on the U S Congress to pass an Act:

> "Expressing the sense of Congress respecting the designation of jazz as a rare and valuable national American treasure."

And concluding:

> "That it is the sense of the Congress that Jazz is hereby designated as a rare and valuable national American treasure to which we should devote our attention, support and resources to make certain it is preserved, understood and promulgated."

It is an extraordinary thing for a Government to try to enshrine a form of art or music in a parliamentary declaration and to set aside resources to ensure its survival. How successful such a scheme may be depends on the nature of the art form and its appeal to the populace.

Jeff Farley has made a serious study of the Act and its consequences. The following summary embodies, in part, the results of his considerations:

> "Few in the industry have criticised the recognition and public subsidy of jazz, but many have found fault with the JPA's definitions of jazz and its history that have dictated this support. While the JPA has essentially continued the practice of shaping jazz through ideas of its place within American culture and society, it has provided immense resources to promote a fixed history and canon for jazz. Specifically, the JPA has promoted jazz as the American music, taking a particular stance on the histories of race and discrimination in the industry and the definitions of authentic jazz that had been sources of disagreement, competition and creativity since the release of the first jazz record in 1917.
>
> Debate amongst writers and musicians continues concerning the 'death' of jazz and its history, and the impact that these have on the current industry.
>
> While I have argued that these issues are important, I have emphasised that the health of jazz lies not in one definitive,

and 'correct' history or canon, but in a plurality of perspectives on jazz history. Jazz history is not now, nor has it ever been, an entirely fixed entity, but rather a process by which jazz has evaluated itself and its tradition to shape the present and future of the music. This is a process that by nature cannot 'die.' Discussions are ongoing concerning issues of race, national identity, cultural value, and musical authenticity and innovation that address jazz as an American music or as a democratic music. These discussions, and the structure that has emerged as a result of the JPA, continue to have a profound effect on lives of musicians and the state of the industry."

One might argue that the survival of an art form cannot be sustained by such national edicts and financial support, but Farley's commentary demonstrates the difficulties when authorities seek to regulate the life of an art form that is so ill-defined.

In addition, Farley clearly identifies that jazz has become an industry struggling to compete with other forms of public entertainment (including the descendants of the blues) and supported by

Academic institutions that control and maintain its characteristics.

What is Jazz?

We all know what it is; don't we? It is an ill-defined, rather old-fashioned form of popular music, supported by enthusiasts, that appeals to a minority of record buyers and concert goers.

In 1926 Herbert Osgood, author of the first history of jazz, predicted that:

> "In another ten years, twenty years, we shall know its fate. And if, as is not unlikely, it withers and dies, still only the popular dance music of the day, to be succeeded by some new form that catches the popular fancy, at least the honour of having been the first and only original art that the United States of America has brought forth in a century and a half of trying can never be taken away from it."

As I suggested in an earlier work, whatever one might think about this debate, it seems clear that at least in the United States, jazz is now dependent on the academies for sustenance and will probably remain so. There is no reason why jazz should not die. Ragtime, before it, declined until it was hardly known by the so-called Swing Generation. (It reappeared briefly in the 1970's due to its appearance in a modified form in a Hollywood movie and it has since been adopted by a growing number of performers.) Jazz is clearly not yet dead. If it did transpire there would still be a need for historians to ponder its fate.

Blues is Blues in 2020

It is difficult to predict the future of its blues-based relatives, but they have cemented a place in the public consciousness. Like bebop the tail of the blues animal has wagged in a number of directions.

Writing for the Encyclopedia Britannica Ed. Ward demonstrated the difficulty of defining the popular perceptions R& B:

> "Perhaps the most commonly understood meaning of the term is as a description of the sophisticated urban music that had been developing since the 1930s, when Louis Jordan's small combo started making blues-based records with humorous lyrics and upbeat rhythms that owed as much to boogie woogie as to classic blues forms. This music, sometimes called jump blues, set

a pattern that became the dominant Black popular music form during and for some time after World War II. Among its leading practitioners were Jordan, Amos Milburn, Roy Milton, Jimmy Liggins, Joe Liggins, Floyd Dixon, Wynonie Harris, Big Joe Turner, and Charles Brown. While many of the numbers in these performers' repertoires were in the classic 12-bar A-A-B blues form, others were straight pop songs, instrumentals that were close to light jazz, or pseudo-Latin compositions. Within this genre there were large-group and small-group rhythm and blues. The former was practiced by singers whose main experience was with big bands and who were usually hired employees of bandleaders such as Lucky Millinder (for whose band Harris sang) or Count Basie (whose vocalists included Turner and Jimmy Witherspoon). The small groups usually consisted of five to seven pieces and counted on individual musicians to take turns in the limelight. Thus, for instance, in Milton's group, Milton played drums and sang, Camille

Howard played piano and sang, and the alto and tenor saxophonists (Milton went through several of them) each would be featured at least once. Another hallmark of small-group rhythm and blues was the relegation of the guitar, if indeed there was one, to a time-keeping status, because guitar soloing was considered "country" and unsophisticated. The most extreme Moore's Three Blazers and in his subsequent work as a bandleader; in both cases the band consisted of piano, bass and guitar, but solos almost totally were handled by Brown on the guitar.

....By mid-decade rhythm and blues had come to mean black popular music that was not overtly aimed at teenagers, since the music that was becoming known as Rock and Roll sometimes featured lyrics that concerned first love and parent-child conflict, as well as a less subtle approach to rhythm. Many vocal groups, therefore, were considered rock-and-roll acts, as were performers such as Little Richard and Hank Ballard and the Midnighters. Because the distinction between rock and roll and rhythm and blues was not based on any hard-and-fast rules, most performers issued records that fit in both categories. Moreover, some vocalists who were later considered jazz performers — in particular, Dinah Washington — also appeared on the rhythm-and-blues charts, and a steady stream of saxophone-led instrumentals firmly in the rhythm-and-blues tradition continued to be produced by performers such as Joe Houston, Chuck Higgins, and Sam ("The Man") Taylor but were considered rock and roll and were often used as theme music by disc jockeys on rock-and-roll radio.

...The term RHYTHM AND BLUES, however, attained a new meaning thanks to the British bands that followed in the wake of the Beatles. Most of these groups, notably the Rolling Stones, played a mixture of Chicago blues and Black rock and roll and described their music as rhythm and blues. Thus, the Who, although a quintessential mod rock band, advertised their early performances as "Maximum R&B" to attract an audience. Although bands that followed this generation—John Mayall's Blues Breakers and Fleetwood Mac, for example—called themselves blues bands, rhythm and blues remained the rubric for the Animals, Them, the Pretty Things, and others. Today a band that advertises itself as rhythm and blues is almost certainly following in this tradition rather than that of the early pioneers."

And what about Funko pop, HipHop, Art Rock, Country Rock, Doo-Wop, Heavy Metal, Rockabilly, Psychedelic Rock? And it all seems a long way back to the blues of Buddy Bolden or to W. C. Handy. Perhaps just as happened to jazz the word blues continues to change its meaning.

Jazz and the blues have travelled a long way together. The future is uncertain.

"All music is folk music. I never heard no horse sing!"
- Louis Armstrong

Epilogue: The Long History of Blue

(An Etymological Perspective}

"The adjective blue has long been used to signify, of a person, the heart, a feeling, etc., depressed, sorrowful, miserable. It was originally a metaphorical use of blue meaning, of the skin, bruised, as in the expression black and blue, discoloured by bruises.

This is explicit in the first known instance of this usage, which is found in Merlin, a Middle-English metrical version of the French romance Estoire de Merlin, completed in the first half of the 15th century by Henry Lovelich, a London skinner; this romance tells that after Arthur's time a great plague gave rise to the name of "Bloye breteyne" (= "Blue Britain") because the British people's "hertes bothe blew and blak they were" (= "hearts both blue and black they were") with sorrow.

The English poet Geoffrey Chaucer (circa 1342-1400) used the metaphor in The Compleynt of Mars (circa 1385).

Ye lovers, that lye in any drede,
Fleeth, lest wikked tonges yow espye.
Lo, yond the sunne, the candel of jelosye!
Wyth teres blewe and with a wounded herte
Taketh your leve.

In contemporary English:

You lovers that are in fear, flee, lest wicked tongues
discover you.
Behold the sun yonder, the candle of jealousy!
With blue tears and with wounded heart, take your
leave.

The adjective blue is also used to signify, of a period, event, circumstance etc., depressing, dismal. In The Short French Dictionary (3rd edition – London, 1690), the Swiss-born lexicographer Guy Miège (1644-circa 1718) wrote: 'Twill be a blue day for him, ce Jour là lui sera fatal. [= that day will be fatal to him]." [lxvii]

———————-

ABOUT THE AUTHOR

Daniel Hardie started playing cornet in a boy's brass band at age 8, later played flute, then drum and bugle at High School, and after graduating in History and Psychology at Sydney University, played clarinet in the Paramount Jazz Band - the house band at the Sydney Jazz Club of which was a founder member. He has a fascination for old boats and jazz history.

Since 2004 he has been Convenor and Historical Director of the *Buddy Bolden Revival Orchestra* dedicated to performance of music of the Elemental Jazz era (1897/1907) with authentic instrumentation

He is the author of:

The Loudest Trumpet: Buddy Bolden and the Early History of Jazz, 2000.

Exploring Early Jazz: The Origins and Evolution of the New Orleans Style, 2002.

The Ancestry of Jazz: A Musical Family History, 2004.

The Birth of Jazz: Reviving the Music of the Bolden Era, 2007.

Jazz Historiography; The Story of Jazz History Writing, 2013.

Jazz and the Jazz Age; Searching for Meaning in a Word, 2020.

Daniel Hardie has also published a number of works and journal articles in the field of Maritime History. He is a maritime painter and has exhibited paintings of heritage maritime subjects in Sydney and other major Australian cities.

End Notes

---

[1] 1917 - Variety - Oct. 19 "Blues Are Blues, They Are" Says Expert In "Blues" Case

[2] THE "BLUES" AS FOLK-SONGS by Dorothy Scarborough

[3] The Dolly Sisters = a vaudeville dancing team

[4] Lomax A. *Mister Jelly Roll* p62

[5] Hardie D *The Ancestry of Jazz* iUniverse 2004

[6] Patterson William Morris *"The Rhythm of Prose - An Experimental Investigation of Individual Difference in The Sense of Rhythm"* 1916 NY Columbia University Press

[7] Kingsley Walter *"Whence Comes Jazz"* THE SUN. (New York [N.Y.]) 1916-1920, August 05, 1917, Section 3, Page 3, Image 23

[9] Thomson Virgil American Mercury August 1924

[10] Gushee L. *The Nineteenth-Century Origins of Jazz* Black Music Research Journal Volume 14, #1 (Spring 1994) p167

[11] Karl Gert Zur Heide in his article about his interview with Charlie Elgar published in the

quarterly Dutch journal Names and Numbers Issue No 24 July 2020 (email to chofmann@hetnet.nl)

[12] Osgood H. *"So This is Jazz"* 1926 Boston, Little Brown

[13] Singleton J. *Keep It Real, The Life Story of James "Jimmy" Palao "The King of Jazz"* –

[14] Frank and Burt Leighton *Origin Of "Blues" (or Jazz)* Variety Jan 6 1922

[15] Hardie D. *The Ancestry of Jazz* iUniverse 2004 p311 Lincoln NE

[16] Scarborough Dorothy THE "BLUES" AS FOLK-SONGS 1916 - FOLK LORE SOCIETY OF TEXAS

[17] Lomax A. *Mr Jelly Roll* p 89

[18] Charters S. Jazz: New Orleans 1968

[19] Marquis D. *In Search of Buddy Bolden 1978*/1993 p 110

[20] Extract from "*The Ancestry of Jazz: A Musical Family History*" D. Hardie 2004

[21] Marquis op cit p 100

[22] Jazz Archivist 1959

[23] Marquis op cit p 100

[24] For an excellent analysis of the Funky Butt Blues story see Hobson B. "Buddy Bolden's Blues" The Jazz Archivist Vol XXI 2008

[25] This project is described in Hardie *D The Birth of Jazz: Reviving the Music of the Bolden Era*

[26] David Sager. *Unraveling the Dawn of Recorded Jazz* the Jazz Archivist Volume XXX, 2017

[27] Shaw Arnold *The Jazz Age* 1986 p112

[28] van der Merwe P. *Evolution of the Popular Style 1992* p 117

[29] van der Merwe op cit1992 p 183

[30] https://www.visitthedelta.com/blues-trail

[31] Lynn Abbott, Doug Seroff, *The Original Blues The Emergence of the Blues in African American Vaudeville 2019*

[32] Hardie *D.The Ancestry of Jazz p152*

[33] The "Blues" as Folk-Songs by Dorothy Scarborough

Folk Lore Society of Texas 1916.

[34] Roberts J.S. The Latin Tinge

[35] See Wardlaw Gayle V. *Chasing That Devil Music* 1998 p 196ff

[36] Hardie D. *The Ancestry of Jazz.* p133

[37] Sheet Music Review Feb 21 1924

[38] Alteratively called Tangana, Habanera, Tresillo based on the rhythm patterns caused by banging two sticks together.

[39] Circle Record. 1682 A

[40] New Orleans Jazz and Caribbean Music 2002 (www.prjc.org)

[42] Chapman, Gary. *The Dolly Sisters: Icons of the Jazz Age* . Edditt Publishing. Kindle Edition.

17 Madrid A. L. and Moore R.D. *Danzon: Circum-Carribean Dialogues in Music and Dance.* NY OUP 2013 p42

18 See Tim Brooks New Orleans' First Record Label: Louis "Bebe" Vasnier and the Louisiana Phonograph Company, 1891 Association for Recorded Sound Collections Conference New Orleans paper 2010

19 Suhor C. dixielandjazz@ml.islandnet.com Wed Oct 28 21:07:56 PDT 201

20 An untuned instrument that is made from a gourd that has been carved or notched to create a ridged surface. The guiro is played by scraping the surface with a stick. Modern guiros are made of materials such as plastic, metal and wood.

[44] By Robert Cole and J. Rosamond Johnson

[45] Sager D. The *Buddy Bolden Cylinder Melt Down: Presaging the Jazz Band on*

[46] That tune is based on the song *Under the Bamboo Tree* by Bob Cole and Rosamond Johnson.

[47] Hardie D. The *Ancestry of Jazz : A Musical Family History*

[48] Sublette N. *Cuba and Its Music*

[49] Kelly J. "*Blues and bop from deep in the soul*" Irish times April 15 2000. 01:00

[50] Biswas G. *Jazz and its Evolution* Academia.edu December 5 2020

[51] For a deeper treatment of its origins go to Scott DeVeaux *Bop*

[52] AU Essays. (November 2018). Music Essays - History of Rhythm and Blues. Retrieved from https://www.auessays.com/essays/music/history-rhythm-blues.php?vref=1

[53] "*WHAT IS A JASS BAND?*" by Gill. - RAGTIME REVIEW - MARCH 191

[54] Probably Jonathan Townley Crane (June 18, 1819 – February 16, 1880) an American clergyman, author and abolitionist.

[55] ENIGMATIC FOLKSONGS OF THE SOUTHERN UNDERWORLD.MISS GILDA GRAY'S "BLUES" AROUSE A DISCUSSION CONCERNING THEIR QUESTIONABLE ORIGIN 1919 - CURRENT OPINION -Sept.

[56] Sargeant W. *"Jazz: Hot and Hybrid,"*1938/1975 pp160/161

[57] Daniel Hardie *The Ancestry of Jazz* p145

[58] Koenig K. *Jazz in Print* p15

[59] This refers to the minstrel shows that portray happy negroes singing on the plantation.

[60] The Sea Islands off the coast of Georgia.

[61] 1899 - New England Magazine - Jan.
Hymns of The Slave And The Freedman - By William E. Barton, D. D.

[62] Carl Engel. " Jazz: A Musical Discussion" -1922 August - Atlantic Monthly

[63] Jazz Music And Its Relation To African Music By Nicholas G. Taylor Of Sierra Leone, South Africa. - Musical Courier 1922 June 1

[64] Koenig op cit p370

[65] https://www.diffen.com/difference/Blues_vs_Jazz

[66] Hardie D. The Ancestry of Jazz p187

[lxvii] Excerpt from the internet site: https://wordhistories.net

Made in the USA
Columbia, SC
25 April 2022

59455781R00104